Edward Lawton Moss

Shores of the Polar Sea

A Narrative of the Arctic Expedition of 1875-6

Edward Lawton Moss

Shores of the Polar Sea
A Narrative of the Arctic Expedition of 1875-6

ISBN/EAN: 9783337330552

Printed in Europe, USA, Canada, Australia, Japan

Cover: Foto ©Andreas Hilbeck / pixelio.de

More available books at **www.hansebooks.com**

SHORES
OF
THE POLAR SEA

A NARRATIVE OF

THE ARCTIC EXPEDITION OF 1875-6

BY
DR. EDWARD L. MOSS, H.M.S. "Alert"

ILLUSTRATED BY
Sixteen Chromo-Lithographs and numerous Engravings
From Drawings made on the spot by the Author

London:
MARCUS WARD & CO., 67 & 68, CHANDOS STREET, STRAND
AND ROYAL ULSTER WORKS, BELFAST
1878

PREFACE.

I PLACE these Sketches in the hands of my Publishers, believing that careful chromo-lithographic fac-similes of them will convey a fuller and perhaps more novel idea of Arctic scenery than any rendering in black and white. As Sketches from Nature, they, for obvious reasons, illustrate rather the scenery of our Expedition than its leading events; the latter are the prerogative of the Historian, and do not come within the scope of a Sketch-book, in which the letterpress is subordinate, and intended merely to connect and describe the pictures. Whatever may be the artistic value of the Sketches—and they lay claim to none—they are at least perfectly faithful efforts to represent the face of Nature in a part of the world that very few can ever see for themselves.

EDWARD L. MOSS.

2nd February, 1877.

CONTENTS.

CHAPTER I.

Entering the Arctic Circle—Continuous Daylight—Dispersion of the Squadron—Rendezvous at Godhavn—The Lost Norse Settlements—Embarkation of Eskimo Dogs and their Driver—Ascent of Hills at Disco—The "LYNGE-MARKEN"—A Paradise for Botanists—Education at Disco—Parting from the Valorous—Proven—Sanderson's Hope—The "North Water"—Northern Limit of Human Habitation—Melville Bay—Northumberland and Hakluyt Islands, . . . 9

CHAPTER II.

Classic Ground—A Ramble over the "Doige Mountains"—Foulke Fiord—The Mer de Glace—Pack Ice—The First Check—Hayes' Sound—Twin Glacier Valley—Charged by a Berg—Varying Fortunes—Walrus, . . . 15

CHAPTER III.

A Haul of the Dredge—Norman Lockyer Island—Traces of an Eskimo Exodus—Midnight on the 12th August—Mysterious Cairns—Forcing the Tidal Barrier—"Kane's Open Polar Sea"—Hannah Island—Grant Land Reached—Musk Oxen—"Discovery's" Winter Quarters, . . . 21

CHAPTER IV.

The Ships Part Company—Robeson Channel—Strange Ice—Lincoln Bay—A Gale—A Rush North—The "Alert" reaches a Latitude never before attained by Ship, and enters a Polar Sea—Precarious Position—Disappointment—No Land to the North—Perennial Ice—Altered Prospects—Autumn Sledging—Pioneering—Dog-sledging—Romance and Reality, . . . 27

CHAPTER V.

Exploration to the Westward—Dumb-bell Bay—A Seal—Search for Game—Lonely Lake—Fish in the Lake—A Gale—Return of the Boat Party—An Opportunity fortunately lost—The Expedition becomes the most Northern—Depots sent forward—Frost-bite Range—Attempts to communicate with H.M.S. "Discovery"—Unexpected Difficulties—Soft Snow—Sunset—Preparations for Winter—The Snow Town—Building Snow Houses—Twilight Walk Shoreward, . . . 32

CHAPTER VI.

End of Twilight—Moonlight—Daily Life in Winter Quarters—Condensation—Breakfast—Morning Prayers—Outdoor Work—Exercise—The Ladies' Mile—A Walk to Flagstaff Point—Sounds from the Pack—Optical Phenomena—Dinner—Our Cat "Pops"—Occupation during Winter—Mock Moons—"Sally"—The Darkness, . . . 40

CHAPTER VII.

Winter Climate—Preservative Effect of Cold—Falling Temperature—Unprecedented Cold—Extreme Low Temperature not Unendurable—A Visitor from the Shore—Cold v. Vitality—Sudden Changes—A Breeze from the South—Warm Wind Aloft—Danger from East Wind—Dawn—Brilliant Effect of Low Sunlight—Lemming—Sunrise—Preparations for Spring—Snowshoes—Our Prospects—Motion of the Floe—A Tidal Wave, . . . 46

CHAPTER VIII.

The Sledging Campaign Opens—A Push for the "Discovery"—Petersen Breaks Down—Shelter in a Snowdrift—Difficulties in Retreat—A First of April Chase—Programme of Spring Sledging—Limited Hopes—Departure of Main Detachments—Double Banking—The Camp—A Night in a Tent—A Typical Floeberg—The Hare's Sanctuary—Coat of Arms—Castle Floe—Parhelia—Road-finding in the Fog—Mirage—A Crevasse, . . . 53

CHAPTER IX.

News from the "Discovery"—Sickness—Petersen's Death and Burial—The Relief of the Northern Detachment—The most Northern Grave—The March to 83° N. Lat—Its Results—The Advance of the Season—Anxiety for the Safety of the Western Party—Its Return—Two Hundred Miles to the West—Further Efforts Poleward Hopeless, . . . 62

CHAPTER X.

Arctic Summer—Flowers and Butterflies—Feathered Visitors—A Strange Shot—Deceptive Game Tracks—The Land Ransacked—No Vestige of Man—Nature's Records—The Raised Beaches—The Break-up—Farewell to Floeberg Beach—Running the Gauntlet—Robeson Channel Ice-drift—A "Nip"—Walled in by Floebergs—Escape—Re-union with the "Discovery," 69

CHAPTER XI.

Serious News—The North Greenland Detachments—The Missing Sledge-crews—Drifting with the Polar Pack—A Forced March of Thirty-two Hours—"Chatel's Grotto" and the "Coal Mine"—Climate Past and Present—The Return Southward—A Pool in Kennedy Channel—Race against Winter—New Ice—Out Fires—The North Water at Last—The "Pandora's" Depôt—News from Home—Conclusion, ... 75

List of Illustrations.

CHROMOGRAPHS.

		PAGE
I.—	Godhavn Harbour, Disco Island, July 10, 1875,	12
II.—	Foulke Fiord and the Inland Ice of Greenland, July 28, 1875,	16
III.—	Musk Ox Hunt, Discovery Harbour, Midnight, August 25, 1875,	24
IV.—	Floeberg Beach and the Polar Sea, looking North from the Crest of Cape Rawson, July, 1876,	28
V.—	Winter Quarters *Outside*, from the Floes Astern of H.M.S. "Alert," December, 1875,	36
VI.—	The Deck: Morning Inspection and Prayers,	40
VII.—	Winter Quarters *Inside* H.M.S. "Alert"—The Wardroom,	44
VIII.—	Lunar Haloes,	48
IX.—	The Dawn of 1876. H.M.S. "Alert" in Winter Quarters,	48
X.—	The "Alert" in Winter Quarters, from amongst the Barrier Bergs, March, 1876,	52
XI.—	Winter Quarters, from amongst the Floebergs, looking South, March, 1876,	56
XII.—	A Floeberg, Simmon's Island, April, 1876,	56
XIII.—	On the Northern March, April 8, 1876,	60
XIV.—	The Most Northern Grave, June, 1876,	64
XV.—	Back from the Farthest North,	68
XVI.—	The Last of the Palæocrystic Floe, Kane's Open Polar Sea, Cape Constitution, Franklin and Crozier Islands in the Distance, August 20, 1876,	80

SKETCHES.

	PAGE		PAGE
Sanderson's Hope .	12	Effect of Extreme Cold on a Candle,	39
Eskimo Boy with Fish,	14	Return from a Winter Walk,	42
Twin Glacier Valley,	18	Examining Thermometer: Minus 73°4,	47
Our White Cat "Pops,"	19	Camp of Sledge Party,	56
Walrus,	20	The Day's March Done,	58
Eskimo Tent-Circles,	22	Crevasse near Cape Joseph Henry,	60
Cape Hawkes,	23	Mirage, 7th April, 1875.	61
Cairns on Washington Irving Island,	24	Petersen's Grave,	63
View from the Top of Hannah Island,	25	The North Coast of Greenland,	68
Head of Musk Ox,	26	Running the Gauntlet,	73
Dragged at the Heels of a Dog-team,	31	Eskimo Bird-Shelter,	74
A Ravine in the Stratified Ice,	31	Chatel's Grotto,	79
Inside the Unifäler House,	36	Allman Bay,	82
Building Snow Houses,	38	Device on Delft-ware of the Expedition,	83

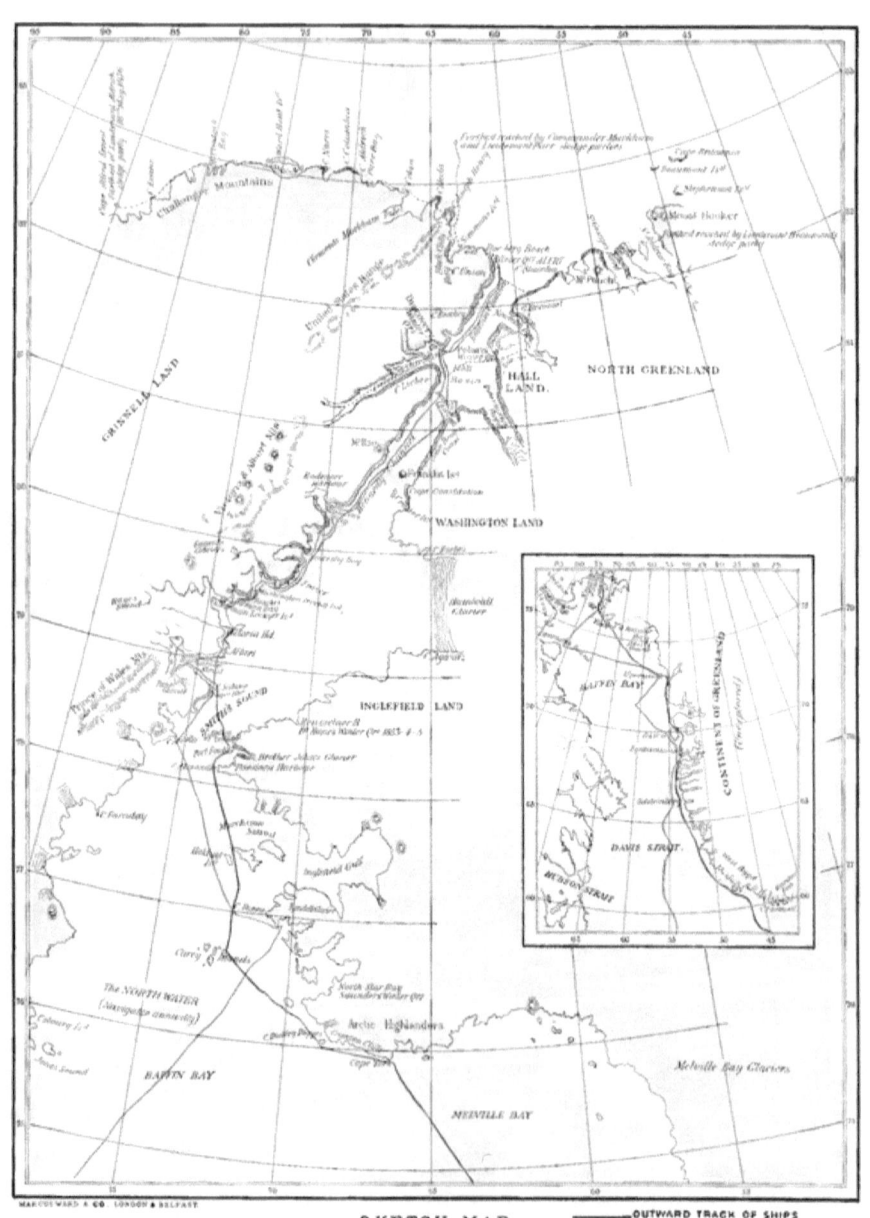

SHORES OF THE POLAR SEA.

CHAPTER I.

Entering the Arctic Circle—Continuous Daylight—Dispersion of the Squadron—Rendezvous at Godhavn—The Lost Norse Settlements—Embarkation of Eskimo Dogs and their Drivers—Ascent of Hills at Disco—The "Lyngmarken"—A Paradise for Botanists—Inhumation at Disco—Parting from the Valorous—Proven—Sanderson's Hope—The "North Water"—Northern Limit of Human Habitation—Melville Bay—Northumberland and Hakluyt Islands.

THE ARCTIC EXPEDITION of 1875 left England on 29th May, crossed the Atlantic to Davis Straits in a succession of storms, and entered the Arctic regions on 4th July. It sailed with orders to "attain the highest northern latitude, and, if possible, reach the Pole."

In old times, when voyages were longer than in these days of steam, a nautical frolic on crossing "the Line" helped to break the monotony of many a tedious passage. This time-honoured custom is slowly becoming a thing of the past. When it is gone, there will be little in sea or sky to make crossing the Equator in any way remarkable. The Tropic Zones are no better defined, and one can sail into or out of them without experiencing a single impressive sensation. But the Arctic Circle has obvious boundaries. A conspicuous change in the ordinary habits of nature warns the traveller that he is leaving the hospitable realms of earth behind him, and entering a region full of new experiences. Here familiar light and darkness cease to alternate, morning and evening no longer make the day, and in proportion as the latitude increases, day and night become mere figures of speech.

While our two ships steamed northward along the west shores of Greenland, the novel charm of constant daylight was felt by every one. We all had our own ideas of what Arctic summer would be like, but ideas drawn from books rarely remain unchanged when brought face to face with reality. Although the passage into perpetual day was of course gradual, yet it was quite rapid enough to upset all regular habits. Most of us observed sadly irregular hours, but one energetic fellow-voyager, bent on making the most of his opportunities, stopped up for three days at a stretch.

Our squadron consisted of H.M.SS. "Alert," "Discovery," and "Valorous," the latter vessel accompanying the Expedition as far as Disco, for the purpose of helping it so far northwards with its heavy stock of three years' provisions and fuel. On entering Davis Straits no one of the ships had the least idea where the others were. They had been separated in a cyclone on 13th June, and had crossed the Atlantic independently. Fortunately, however, all three turned up almost simultaneously off the west coast of Greenland. Four days before crossing the Arctic Circle, the "Alert" and "Discovery" met under the rugged coast near Godhaab. As the ships approached, each anxiously scanned the other to see what damage had been done by the Atlantic storms. Boats soon passed from ship to ship, and it was amusing to note how both men and officers of either ship (the writer included) already placed the firmest faith in their own vessel, and underrated the seaworthiness of her consort. It was positively quite disappointing to find that the "Discovery's" spars were all right, and that she, like ourselves, had lost but one boat. Of course we congratulated each other on our good fortune; and good fortune it was, for our light, beautifully built boats could not be replaced, and few ships, heavily laden both below and on deck as ours were, would have passed through such weather without more serious loss.

The deep fiords and treeless valleys of this west coast own a little known and mysterious history. Nine centuries ago, numerous bands of Norsemen, led by Eric and his restless sons Leif and Thorwald, found congenial homes on these lonely shores. For three hundred years or more their thriving settlements studded the coast; and while their southern brethren were building Gothic shrines in England, Normandy, and Flanders, the thirteen bishops of the East and West Bygds reared humbler fanes at Foss and Gardar, Steinnaes and Solfjall, and many another spot uncertain now. The sites of the settlements are still marked by scattered ruins, many of them covered by the encroaching tide. These, together with a few inscriptions, and a bronze church bell, are all that remain of the Norsemen. For in the middle of the fourteenth century the colonies vanished suddenly and for ever. Then came the dark ages of Greenland; and when the Moravian missionaries landed in 1721, close to the spot where we met the "Discovery," a pagan race from the north-west peopled the coast, and knew nothing of the Norsemen. But as they sat crouched round their seal-oil lamps and turf fires in the long winter evenings, they told many a vague traditionary story of tall fierce men, with fair hair and strangely long noses, that had gone away no one knew where, northward, or perhaps to the mountains far inland.

Before the Expedition left England, an arrangement through the Danish Government had been made for the supply of a suitable number of Eskimo dogs for our dog-sledges, and information about them was to be received at the settlement of Disco. That port had been selected as a rendezvous for the ships in case they should be separated, and there H.M.S. "Valorous" would transfer the stores she had carried out for the Expedition. Accordingly, the ships steamed in under the high buttressed cliffs of Disco Island to the little land-locked harbour of Godhavn, and anchored off the village of Leively on the afternoon of 6th July. The "Valorous" had arrived there the day before, and the three ships of our squadron, surrounded by a crowd of native kayaks, and with boats constantly passing to and fro, gave the quiet harbour an unwontedly business-like appearance. Not that Leively is always in the state of repose in which we found it. Whaling ships not uncommonly call in on their way to the western fishing-grounds, and five had visited Godhavn early in that season. At first sight it seems reasonable to ask, Why had not the Arctic Expedition gone northward as early as the whaling ships, so as to make the most of the short open season? But it will be remembered that, in such a channel as Smith's Sound, the separation of the ice-pack from its shores only commences when the formation of the North Water in Baffin's Bay gives the ice room to drift, and that in the far northern regions of Kennedy and Robeson Channels, through which the Expedition hoped to penetrate, no ice motion could occur, until room had been made for it by drift, crushing together, or disintegration of the southern floes. Even after the break-up had travelled far northwards, undue precipitancy would be disastrous. Much of our precious fuel might be expended in pushing through, and being checked by ice which, a little later on, would move down, and leave an uninterrupted passage to the North. Accordingly, we had plenty of time for all that had to be done at Disco. Every available space was filled with coal. Casks and cases of provisions covered the upper deck. Twenty splendid dogs were embarked in charge of our intelligent and trustworthy Eskimo dog-driver "Fred," who was here entered on the books of the Expedition. Chronometers were rated, and magnetic deflections noted. And the first camping-out was done by a party to the site of the supposed meteorolites at Ovifak. After working hours the high basaltic cliffs beyond the harbour were irresistibly attractive. From the deck of the ship it was easy to plan routes to the top, but not everyone who tried the climb succeeded. A bold detour to the left was eventually found the easiest way up, and a cairn on a noble bluff over the "Lyngemarken" records our visit. Nothing could be more picturesque than these fine cliffs, bathed in evening sunlight that caught every pinnacle and ridge, but left the ravines in shadow. Patches of last winter's snow, here and there brilliantly pink with the red snow-plant, lay in the hollows and watercourses. The green "Lyngemarken," or heath-field, below is perhaps the most luxurious spot inside the Arctic Circle, and is well known as a paradise for botanists. A small stream running through its centre is said to flow for the greater part of the year. During our visit its banks were lined with soft green vegetation, bordering miniature groves of dwarf willow three feet high, and the rocky flats beyond were rich with purple rhododendron. The Eskimo shooting season was over, but a few ptarmigan still croaked amongst the neighbouring rocks; their numbers were too few to reward our sportsmen for the trouble of climbing after them.

The little settlement is built upon a bare rocky promontory—an island at high tide—forming the south side of the harbour. It consists of two or three substantial wooden houses inhabited by the Danish officials, a few storehouses, and a dozen "igloos," or mud huts, occupied by the natives of the place, Eskimo in dress and mode of life, but often with the slender forms, fair hair, and freckled complexion that mark European admixture. On some rocks over the centre of the village stands a little black church, unpretending, but efficient—not unfairly representing the moral culture of its congregation. Here, and at all other Danish settlements touched at by the Expedition, the Eskimo appear to have retained all the virtues that Hans Egede found amongst their pagan ancestors, when he and his courageous little band undertook the re-Christianisation of Greenland one hundred and fifty-five years ago. "Hatred and envy, strife and jars, are never heard of amongst them," and "they have a great abhorrence of stealing." Leaving them to live by hunting and fishing, as their fathers did before them, their governors and pastors have succeeded in giving them a civilised education, without making it a roadway for European vices. The contrast between their semi-savage appearance and scholastic accomplishments was sometimes striking. One day a little fellow some six or seven years of age, clad in sealskin, and with his straight black hair lying on his shoulders, clambered on board out of his kayak, with some fresh-caught rock cod for sale, or rather barter, for we had no money. He happened to come into our wardroom, and was shown an illustrated book of birds, in the hope that he would pronounce some of their Eskimo names, but the book chanced to be Danish, and he surprised us by reading it fluently. We were informed that every child in both northern and southern Greenland is taught to read and write, but it is difficult to imagine that there are not exceptions, for the people are scattered in almost isolated families and groups amongst the countless rocky islands of the coast. Godhavn district has two hundred and forty-five inhabitants, distributed in three settlements fifteen miles apart. Their numbers are fast decreasing, and in a few years the last pure-bred Eskimo will have disappeared. Whether the mixed race will be able to hold its own against the unkindness of Nature appears doubtful. Perhaps Greenland is fated to again become a land without inhabitant.

The Expedition left Disco on 15th July, and steamed northward between the island and the mainland. Then, making a short halt at Rittenbenk, it stood down the Waigat. At a distance it seemed as if the whole strait was blocked with icebergs; we, however, found broad leads of water between them, smooth as a mirror, but for an occasional swell, as some great fragment slipped into the sea with a roar like a distant park of artillery. There, with the most earnest wishes for our success, our friends of the "Valorous" bade us adieu. An hour afterwards we found ourselves cruising about amongst the bergs in a thick fog. Every now and then a white mass would be seen gleaming ahead; down would go the helm just in time to avoid collision, and the sound of the sea in the azure hollows along its sides would scarcely be gone when the helm was again hard over to clear another.

It was evidently advisable to wait till the fog lifted, and accordingly the ships were brought up to a berg, and some men despatched to clamber up and secure an ice anchor; but at the first blow of the ice gouge, down slid a great shoulder of the berg, carrying with it one of our men, and nearly overwhelming the boat in its surge. As the water calmed, blue lumps of ice shot up to the surface here and there, and presently "Francombe" bobbed up amongst them swimming vigorously for the boat, chilly, but nothing the worse for his dive.

Next morning the fog disappeared, and, leaving Hare Island on our left, we stood out to sea. Four days afterwards our stock of dogs was completed at Proven, a little settlement where neither dogs nor men seemed over well off for food. Here, too, we embarked the veteran Hans as dog-driver for H.M.S. "Discovery." The records of Kane, Hayes, and Hall have made his name, but not his worth, familiar to every reader. Undeterred by the fate of two out of the three

SANDERSON'S HOPE.

ships in which he had served, he again ventured into Smith's Sound ice. The same evening, steaming towards the low midnight sun, we passed close under the magnificent cliffs of Sanderson's Hope, a perpendicular wall of rock 1000 feet high, cleft by a narrow fiord like the portal of a colossal ruin. We could not but regret that time forbade us to explore its blue recesses.

A mile or two further on, our ships stopped for an hour and secured a sufficient number of "looms" to supply two dinners of fresh food to all hands. The slaughter of the poor birds was most unmerciful, but they made excellent soup and pies, and tasted like hare. Next day, towing the "Discovery" in order to save fuel, we groped our way in a dense fog through a labyrinth of rocks into the harbour of Upernivik, the most northern civilised settlement on the globe.

PLATE I.—GODHAVN HARBOUR, DISCO ISLAND, JULY 10, 1875.—p. 11.

THE Danish settlements on the coast of Greenland are divided into two Inspectorates—a northern and a southern. Godhavn is the head-quarters of the northern. The view is from the rocks above the little village of Leively, looking down on the harbour that gives the district its name. The Lyngmarken cliffs beyond are a fine sample of the southern shores of Disco. A few houses of Danish officials, some store-houses, a church, a school-house, and the huts of the Eskimo make the village.

A pair of Eskimo women—unmarried, as may be seen by their red top-knots—are busy with their laundry work at a pool amongst the glaciated rocks of the foreground.

MELVILLE BAY.

Henceforward we would be beyond the reach of any regular communication with home; accordingly, our last letters were landed to await the departure of the next Danish brig.

Melville Bay lay before us; its dreaded ice once passed, the Expedition might safely count on at least entering Smith's Sound. Our leader determined to take a direct course, and force a way through the "middle pack." For hours not a speck of ice was to be seen. Our ice quartermasters, whose experience was drawn from many a whaling voyage made much earlier in the season, warned us not to be too hopeful; to every enquiry they shook their heads and answered, "Wait a bit and ye'll see ice enou'." And so we did, but it was worn and soft, crumbling at every touch, and with broad lanes of water leading through it in every direction. What it would be if blown together by wind is another question, but, as we found it, the dreaded middle pack was simply despicable. Every one was in the highest spirits. The failure of a bear-hunt did not much disappoint us. Were there not plenty of bears in the Far North? Side by side, or one or other leading, the ships passed full speed between the flat floes, from one placid pool to another, every rope and spar reflected on the water in a complete inverted ship. We would not have believed that mere sea could supply such a thoroughly mirror-like surface. Here too we have our first experience of what sunlight on ice could be. Pink and metallic, green, pale yellow, and violet, the ice lay, far as the eye could reach, like fields of mother-of-pearl. Many of us sat up till the last ice was out of sight, and in the morning we were well in the "North Water."

Anyone who looks back through the logs of the old explorers and whalers in Baffin's Sea, will be struck with the fact that Melville Bay used to be looked upon as a sort of very formidable "Pons Asinorum" at the outset of every voyage. The navigator who had sailed northward safely enough between the Baffin sea-pack and the long stream of ice that flows round the coast of Greenland, often found himself checked by ice, or baffled by wind, when he passed Upernivik and sighted the "Devil's Thumb;" or, if he passed into the grasp of the Bay, he would be paralysed by calms, and the toil of slowly hauling his ship along the land-ice not unfrequently ended in a hasty dock-cutting to avoid a nip, a lost season, or perhaps a fatal crush. In old times the loss of whaling ships in Melville Bay was almost of annual occurrence; but the introduction of steam as a motive power has robbed the Bay of its terrors. Whaling disasters are perhaps as common as ever, but that is only because the fleets of steam-ships which now annually enter the northern ice are compelled to follow the whale into seas even more dangerous than Melville Bay.

Here and at many subsequent points of our voyage, where we had forcible evidence of the value of steam in ice-navigation, we learned to appreciate the work done by the old sailing expeditions. Much that was easy to us would have been impossible to them; and often as we advanced in a perfect calm, or steamed head-to-wind through narrow leads between wheeling fields of ice, we wondered at the distances safely navigated by such ships as the "Hecla" and "Griper," or "Enterprise" and "Investigator," along shores exposed to as heavy Polar ice as any our vessels encountered.

A few Eskimo still inhabit the Greenland shores north of Melville Bay, cut off from all intercourse with their kind by one hundred miles of glacier; these, the Arctic Highlanders of Sir John Ross, amongst whom Kane and Hayes wintered, are undergoing steady diminution. They appear to have fallen back on the southern parts of their territory, and are making their last stand in the neighbourhood of Cape York. Our dog-driver Hans there communicated with his wife's kindred, and through him we learnt that the tribe was now reduced to eighty souls. The object of our visit was to pick up Hans's brother-in-law, but he was absent on a hunting excursion. Leaving them to wonder what brought white men northwards, we continued our course, trying to keep warm a hope that yet another human community, Norse, or at least Eskimo, might possibly be found beyond the threshold of the unknown regions we were so fast approaching. With calm weather and warm sun, giving us a temperature of 40° on deck, we steamed northwards with the utmost possible economy of fuel. A fleet of large icebergs lay along the coast north of Cape York. One time two hundred and thirty were in sight, many of them islands of glacier a thousand feet thick, and looking too large to have come from the adjacent coast.

From this time forwards land was never out of sight. Panoramas of coast-line continually unrolled on one side or the other. A certain sameness of rock and snow necessarily ran through all, but there was a sort of speculative pleasure in watching the changing profile of the next headland, or the gradual opening of some unknown bay. Northwards from Cape York lay the "crimson cliffs of Beverly," owing their colour not to the "red snow" of their glaciers, as in Sir J. Ross's time, but to rich lichens covering their brick-red rocks. The brilliant orange lichens of Cape Dudley-Digges will not be readily forgotten. Passing between the terraced precipices of Northumberland and Hakluyt Islands, we reached the most eastern of the Carey Islands on 27th July. Here a depot of provisions and a boat were landed, forming the first of a series of reserves to be deposited along the route northwards, so as to give some help to our retreating crews, if unhappily the fate of our predecessors should be in store for us. Going and returning from the island in our boats we miserably slaughtered ten eider ducks, swimming about with their young broods. There was no help for it; in the Arctic region "the pot" is peremptory. Even here, however, we were not alone in our cruelty. Looking over the side of the boat into the blue water, numbers of little pink-tipped "clio," like miniature daggers, could be seen eagerly chasing and devouring fluttering black-winged sea-snails almost as large as themselves. Captivity in a tea-cup did not abate their voracity. A victim was no sooner introduced than he was pounced upon, caught by strong sucker-armed tentacles, turned round till the defenceless opening of his shell was opposite his captor's mouth, and pulled out by two sets of sharp hooks, after the manner of a periwinkle with a pin.

CHAPTER II.

Classic Ground—A Ramble over the "Doige Mountains"—Foulke Fiord—The Mer de Glace—Pack Ice—The First Check—Hayes' Sound—Twin Glacier Valley—Charged by a Berg—Varying Fortunes—Walrus.

RECORDS of our advance were to be deposited at Lyttelton Island, for the information of a relief ship which would so far follow us if the Expedition should remain northward for two winters. Accordingly, on the morning of 28th July, our ships anchored off Reindeer Point, Port Foulke. Here we were on ground that must always possess a deep interest for every Arctic traveller. The southern side of our little bay shut in the winter quarters from which Dr. Hayes had brought his ship safely home; out to seaward Lyttelton Island was strewn with remains of the "Polaris," and Rensselaer Harbour, famed as the winter quarters of Dr. Kane, was but thirty miles to the northward. A path, still plainly discernible, led across a gap in the Doige range to the deserted Eskimo settlement of Etah; and if any further inducement was required to make the shore attractive, it was supplied by a little note on our chart, "reindeer plentiful."

Our time for exploration was limited, for the ships would weigh anchor on the return of the main party from Lyttelton Island. Leaving the ship as soon as possible after breakfast, we landed amongst fragments of shore ice which still lined the little bay, and travelled inland up a valley completely bare of snow, and green with saxifrage, willow, and grasses. A rivulet trickled through some marshy ground in its centre, amongst treacherous islands of rich-coloured velvety moss, and occasional broad ripple-marked slabs of red sandstone. The whole ground was covered with footprints of reindeer, but a gentle wind blew up the valley, and left little hope of sighting them. Climbing the hills to the northward to obtain a better view, a broad undulating table-land lay spread out before us, ridges of plutonic rock, like low walls, traversed the country from east to west, and here and there marshy pools, some of them almost deserving the name of lakes, lay in the hollows, and sent little streams winding towards gaps in the coast cliffs. Beyond and below the cliffs lay Smith's Sound, an unbroken expanse of blue, limited westward by snow-clad Ellesmere Land between Capes Isabella and distant Sabine. The strait was, so far, quite open and unencumbered by ice, but away to the northward, where Hayes' Sound interrupted the outline of the coast, a long thin line of pack, the first indication of coming troubles, streaked the horizon. This was bad news to have to report on our return to the ship, but there was no help for it. We turned our backs on it, and struck out inland across the muddy flats in the direction of Foulke Fiord. The Doige Range looked near enough, but an hour's hard walking did not bring it much nearer. Two steep ravines had to be crossed, as well as a stream, which fortunately was in one place bridged by a deep snowdrift that afforded firm footing across. At length the precipitous cliffs of Foulke Fiord were reached at a point close above the deserted settlement of Etah. Looking down into the fiord, large flocks of little auks were seen perched in black and white lines along the ledges.

A small ravine intersects the cliff-edge a little eastward from the "Aukrey," and on the brow over it we came upon two structures, evidently the work of man, puzzling enough at the time, but which we have since learnt to recognise as Eskimo meat *caches* or safes. Each consisted of a pile of stones covering in a long rectangular chamber, left open at one end, but easily closed by a flat stone which lay close by. Both stood in a conspicuous position on the top of a little rise, and were surrounded by lemming and fox marks. A mile further eastward, the cliffs promised a good commanding position for a view, but the rough and undulating hill-tops took us a good while to get over. At length the ascent of the last ridge was commenced, when suddenly a snow-white object appeared over the brow. It was an Arctic hare, the first we had seen. He was evidently astonished at the reappearance of his old enemy, man, and it was not till after he had made a careful examination of us, standing straight up, full length, on his hind feet, that he concluded we were to be avoided. Then off he went, running ten or fifteen paces erect, then a bound or two on all-fours, then erect again, and finally, when he had run some eighty or one hundred yards, he stopped for another look, sitting on his haunches like a dog begging. This time we were ready for him; he presented a steady mark, and his curiosity was fatal to him. On going to pick him up, we came on a low wall of stones roughly piled, nowhere more than two feet high, leading from the cliff-edge on the right, for about eighty yards inland, to a small shallow tarn; it was apparently some Eskimo hunting contrivance, possibly to assist in driving small game to a suitable spot over the cliffs. Amongst the rounded boulders in the margins of the tarn lay a great number of shed antlers of reindeer, some of them broken and moss-grown, half-buried in the mud; others bleached white, but evidently of no great age. The tips of almost all showed marks of having been gnawed by foxes. Some scattered antlers were found on other parts of the hills, but were always numerous round the tarns; every one we met with had horns of various sizes and ages lying about it.

On reaching the summit we were amply rewarded for our expenditure of energy. The prospect was truly magnificent. A thousand feet below, the blue waters of Foulke Fiord lay, rippled with a breeze, under the richly-coloured cliffs of the opposite shore; further on, the flat expanse at the head of the inlet, with Alida Lake, and Brother John's Glacier of Kane, shaped like a great paw, closed in the valley. Beyond and above all, a broad white plain, the vast inland ice of Greenland, lay spread before us. Even at first sight, this sea of ice could not be mistaken for a frozen sea, for its distant horizon was sensibly above our level.

The coast of Greenland, like other western shores, is so subdivided by inlets and fiords, that there are but few places where it is possible to get a good view over any extent of the *mer de glace*. Three or four miles off, as we saw it, its surface seems smooth enough, but it is really so uneven and fissured, that the most persevering attempts to travel inland over it have penetrated but a short distance, after three days' incessant toil. When not checked by labyrinths of crevasses, the travellers have encountered impassable rivers, flowing in icy beds, till they plunged in a cloud of mist into fathomless pits. Enough, however, has been learned to justify the belief, that a continuous mass of ice, many thousand feet deep, loads the whole of Greenland, from the land's end near Cape Farewell, to far north beyond Peterman's fiord, where our Expedition traced its outline behind the coast hills on the shores of the Polar Sea.

The place where we stood afforded an excellent site for a sketch; some bold rocks over the cliffs and a mellow-tinted herbage—principally red-tipped three-cleft saxifrage—supplied a good foreground. Our artistic proceedings were, however, interrupted by the appearance of a little grey fox, attracted doubtless by the dead hare. He seemed perfectly aware of the danger he ran, and never exposed more

PLATE II.—FOULKE FIORD AND THE INLAND ICE OF GREENLAND,
JULY 28, 1875.—p. 16.

FOULKE FIORD is a narrow ice-scooped inlet in the coast of Greenland, at the entrance of Smith's Sound. Hayes made it his winter quarters; and Rensselaer Bay, where Kane spent his three winters, is close to the northward. On the shore of the fiord, and under the red granite cliff in foreground of the picture, a few ruined huts mark the site of the once populous Eskimo village of Etah—the capital of the "Arctic Highlanders." At the head of the fiord an expanse of lake and valley leads to Brother John's Glacier of Kane, stretching down in the shape of a huge paw from the inland ice beyond. This continental ice lies thousands of feet thick over what little is known of the interior of Greenland, and looks like a vast frozen sea, but that its level is sensibly above the horizon.

than his forehead, ears, and eyes over the rocks behind which he had taken up his position. His skin would have made an acceptable addition to our collection; and after waiting some time in hope that he would make a further advance, he was fired at, but missed, and he gave us no opportunity for a second shot.

It was now high time to get back to the ships, so, shouldering a specimen pair of reindeer horns and our hare, we took a direct course across the Doige Range, but found it by no means an easy one, for a steep ravine had to be crossed, and a rapid knee-deep stream waded, before the hills of Reindeer Point were reached. On getting to the ship, we learned that a party of officers from the "Discovery" had been more successful than we were. Landing at the head of the inlet, they had searched the valley below Brother John's Glacier, and climbed the cliffs on its southern side. There they found three reindeer, which led them a severe chase across the glacier. They finally secured one of them, and carried the best parts of the meat to their boat, but not until one of the most active of the party was so much exhausted, that it required the united exertions of the others to keep him awake.

The ice seen northwards from the hills over our anchorage at Port Foulke was met with off Cape Sabine the day after we left, and found to be altogether impenetrable. It was disheartening to see the ships come to a complete stand-still under steam and sail in the very first pack-ice we encountered in Smith's Sound. We were compelled again and again to return and shelter in a little harbour inside some islands three miles south of Cape Sabine. Our prospects seemed sufficiently discouraging. We had only reached the latitude of Dr. Kane's winter quarters, and here was an impassable barrier of ice stretching north and east, as far as we could see from the rocky hills over our harbour of refuge. Our chances of progress were often discussed sitting round the table after dinner, and when one of us, hoping to gain support from opposition, suggested that perhaps we might have to winter here, it was at first treated as a joke, but after half-a-dozen failures to advance, the subject was dropped as altogether too serious for discussion. Four days were spent in fruitless efforts to push through the tongue of pack stretching into Hayes' Sound, and we thus got early experience of the necessity of a continuous coast-line for ice navigation. At length a fine lead of water opened round Cape Sabine into Hayes' Sound. If we could not go north, we might at least go west, and hold ourselves ready to seize any opportunities for advance that the unknown waters of Hayes' Sound might offer.

After three or four hours' rapid steam and sail, in the line of water between the floes and shore, the sound was found to subdivide into a number of narrow inlets. The only available lane of water led into the first of these. As we passed into it, a strange landmark on the top of a long hill on its south side attracted our attention. If we had been in an inhabited latitude, no one would have hesitated to call it a house. We could only suppose it to be a gigantic and singularly square specimen of the boulders which here strew the surface of the country. The inlet did not run far, and we soon found ourselves "brought up" off a broad valley closed in landwards by the union of two large glaciers. The ships were secured inside some rocks to wait for the opening of the ice, which would probably occur next tide. The shores here were virgin ground, and parties were soon organised to explore the valley. It was two miles wide at its sea face, and not far from three in length; precipitous hills rose on either side; along the centre, a stream from the ice above had cut a water-course, in some places as much as eighty feet deep, through the soft yellow sandstone. At the head of the valley, a wall of ice, formed by the junction of two glaciers, stood across it from side to side. The glacier on the right terminated in a perpendicular cliff seventy feet high, excavated along the ground, and with small streams spouting from blue fissures in its wall; that on the left was parallel with the former, but rounded off gradually to a sort of glacis covered with a thin layer of black mud, smelling strongly of decaying vegetable matter. Bunches of dead heather-like Cassiopea cropped up amongst the stones within three feet of the sloping face of ice. The stream came down from an amphitheatre between the glaciers, which, half-a-mile further on, met in a ridge, caused by the right hand glacier being forced up over the left.

We were greatly disappointed at finding no game in the valley; there was not even a ptarmigan or a hare to be seen, though tracks of both were numerous. Every gap in the banks of the watercourse was pitted with the footprints of reindeer or musk oxen. A number of boulders strewed the valley, and every one that was large enough had been used as scratching-posts by musk oxen, as the white wool and brown hair on and around them testified.

A splendid erratic block of red granite, twelve or fifteen feet high, lay in the south side of the valley, and round it a complete trench was worn deep into the ground by the foot prints of musk oxen

TWIN GLACIER VALLEY

as they rubbed themselves against it or stood under it for shelter. This glen was even more fertile than Port Foulke, and would make a delightful winter quarters for an amateur Arctic Expedition. There was plenty of willow, with large well-grown leaves, and in many places the ground was covered with a perfect garden of dwarf flowers; even in the dry parts of the river bed, patches of purple Epilobium covered the sand. We could only account for the absence of game by supposing that the neighbouring valleys were equally rich. An old reindeer antler was picked up, together with the skull of a bear, and at the upper end of the valley some remains of Eskimo "igloos" were discovered, with door posts made of whale ribs.

Our furthest point in Hayes' Sound was reached two days afterwards, and, so far as we could see, the peninsula on our right was not an island. We subsequently saw that it, and the very similar headland next north of it, were parts of the same land, only separated by a curve in the coast with a low hill in the centre. We accordingly ceased to speak of our headlands as Henry and Bache Islands, and returned to their original titles, Capes Albert and Victoria.

At length the long check at Hayes' Sound came to an end. Some southward motion in the ice opened a lead round Cape Albert. It was at once taken advantage of, and when it closed in again the ships were well to the north of the Cape, but, unfortunately, completely imprisoned in close pack drifting steadily southwards, and taking them with it. There was no fixed point to lay hold on. The long wall of horizontally banded cliffs was more than a mile off, and, even if we could have reached it, there did not appear to be any little curve or hollow where we could have held our own. What little we had won seemed slipping from us. There was nothing to be done but wait patiently for the chances of the next tide. "Tea" had been cleared away in the wardroom, and logs were being written up and journals posted, when we were startled by sudden orders on deck. "Full speed ahead!" "Clear away jib!" "Set fore-top sail, top-gallant sail, and foresail!" We rushed on deck, expecting that a

fine lead had opened northwards, but, lo! the ships were still fast in the pack, and drifting right down upon an iceberg two hundred yards long and forty feet above water that crushed through the floes towards us. The "Alert" was directly in its path. Men out on the ice ahead and astern tried to make way, and hauled with ice anchors and tackle; full steam and sail failed to move her. The pack tightened every moment with increasing pressure. The roar of the crushing ice came nearer and nearer. And as the orders "Up screw and up rudders" were given, those of us who were useless on deck went below to see that our messmates' haversacks were ready to be flung out on the ice alongside, if our ship's strong beams should prove unequal to the crush. In solitary possession of the wardroom, and quite undisturbed by the excitement on deck, our white cat "Pops" dozed peacefully in her favourite posture on a chair in front of the stove. When we went on deck again the critical moment had come. The stern was clear of the berg, but the bow was in its direct path. The ice pack, buckling and shovelling in front, caught the fore part of the ship, and pushed her forcibly sternwards, swinging her half round into a stream of ice and water sweeping past the berg. The danger was over, but our jibboom was not four feet from the wall of ice. Such an opportunity of arresting our southward drift was not to be lost. Grappling appliances were all ready, and in a moment both ships were being towed comfortably along in the wake of their old enemy.

The events of next day well illustrate the uncertainties of ice navigation. At 2 a.m. the ships had slowly struggled northwards until they were abeam of Cape Victoria, but there the ice closed in and "nipped" the ships close inshore under the cliffs. Rudder and screw were again raised to save them from the dangerous pressure, which increased till the floes, sliding one under the other, were forced landwards completely under the ship. At that moment nothing could be more unpromising than the prospects of the expedition, and yet, twenty minutes afterwards we were steaming cheerily along through a good lead towards Franklin and Pierce Bay. By breakfast time we had crossed to the north-eastern shore of the bay, and found further progress checked for the time by floes close packed against the rugged headlands to the north. As the ships were secured to the edge of a broad flat floe lying between an island and the high conglomerate cliffs of the mainland, several walrus were seen lying on a fragment of floe about a mile off. Their flesh would make a most valuable store of food for our dogs, who had been living almost exclusively on preserved Australian meat, for they disliked dog biscuit. Accordingly, a whale-boat with a harpoon gun in her bows was lowered and manned. It was necessary to make a long detour. New ice forming in the shadow of the cliffs impeded our progress and rendered a noiseless attack impossible. Our game, however, paid no attention to the noise we made scraping the ice with the oars and breaking a road with a paddle. We soon got close enough to see that there were three of them lying close together. Occasionally one or other would rear himself slowly up, displaying his double-lobed head and long gleaming tusks, scratch his side lazily with his huge flipper, and fling himself down again with a satisfied grunt beside his slumbering companions. They lay on the edge of a floe. We steered for the largest of the three, and at length the broad arrow-head of the harpoon, projecting from the muzzle of the gun, was within five yards of the beast. Then, with the flash, the steel buries itself deep in his side, a stream of blood spurts on the snow, and all three walrus start up and heave themselves upright before plunging into the water, looking as formidable game as any post-diluvian sportsman could desire, but evidently too much frightened to attack. A well-aimed bullet struck our victim's throat and shortened his death-struggle. Ere long the drag on the harpoon line slackened, and the huge carcase was drawn to the surface and towed slowly to the ship. It measured twelve and a-half feet from nose to tail, eleven and a-half in girth. The tusks, eighteen inches from gum to point, gave the creature a savage appearance, but their use was to dig up the molluscs on which he fed, or to hook himself up on to the ice floes. The dogs were not alone in their appreciation of fresh meat. We ourselves found some steaks by no means unpalatable though desperately tough, and for some days walrus liver figured upon our breakfast-table.

CHAPTER III.

A Haul of the Dredge—Norman Lockyer Island—Traces of an Eskimo Exodus—Midnight on 12th August—Mysterious Cairns—Forcing the Tidal Barrier—"Kane's Open Polar Sea"—Hannah Island—Grant Land Reached—Musk Oxen—"Discovery's" Winter Quarters.

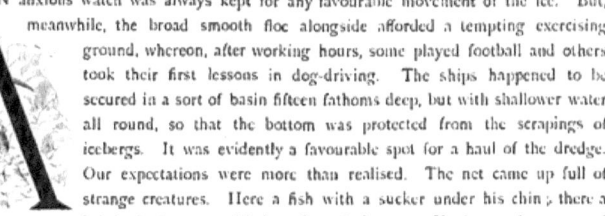

AN anxious watch was always kept for any favourable movement of the ice. But, meanwhile, the broad smooth floe alongside afforded a tempting exercising ground, whereon, after working hours, some played football and others took their first lessons in dog-driving. The ships happened to be secured in a sort of basin fifteen fathoms deep, but with shallower water all round, so that the bottom was protected from the scrapings of icebergs. It was evidently a favourable spot for a haul of the dredge. Our expectations were more than realised. The net came up full of strange creatures. Here a fish with a sucker under his chin; there a brittle feather star with long branched arms. He has to be extracted most carefully from the bag, and supplied with some cotton to grasp before being consigned to our naturalist's ever-ready bottle. Next comes a *Terebratula*, or lamp shell, anchored by a strange chance to a fossil *Terebratula* drifted from some neighbouring rock. Here are pale vermilion-coloured antlers of *Escharella*, and delicate lacework of *Retepore Polyzoa*, and here, perhaps greatest prize of all, a little calcareous sponge with a double frill glistening like spun glass. The dredging operations were continued far into the nominal night, and, after a little necessary rest, we started to explore the island. A steep wall of ice-foot encircling the land disputed our inroad. Clambering up over it, we were at once struck with the terraced condition of the shores. On the north side of the island especially, the ridges rose one over the other in long horizontal waves to the number of twenty or more. Even on the highest, sea shells were to be picked up. Each ridge was tipped here and there with little mounds of yellow clay, sometimes in lines at right angles to the ridges. The shore was very barren; a few little grey tufts of grass, or Draba, found root in the mounds of yellow clay, all the rest was small stones weathered into sharp points like cinders.

When we reached the northern shores of the island, a number of conspicuous white objects strewn along the lower terraces excited our curiosity. They were bones of walrus and seal, much broken evidently by the hand of man, but fragile and moss-grown with age. Some long-vanished tribe had doubtless found this lonely island a rich hunting-ground. The western point of the island was covered with the foundations of a complete town. In some places mere rings of stones had served to keep down the edges of summer tents of skins; in others, rectangular enclosures three yards broad, with excavated floor and with traces of porch opening seawards, gave unmistakable evidence of more permanent habitation. Deep carpets of velvety moss found rich soil in the floors of the huts, which had doubtless been no cleaner than that of modern Eskimo. A little further inland we came upon a bird-shelter, such as the natives of Danish Greenland still use to encourage geese and duck to settle on their shores. It consisted of four stones piled together like a miniature "Druid's altar," so as to form a chamber large enough to shelter a nest. Generations of eider duck had been hatched in it in security since the last wild hunter left the shore. When we found it, it held a deep nest of eider down with three eggs, fresh, but cold, probably belonging to a duck we had killed before landing. The traces of former human habitation found on this island, as well as at other places further northwards, seemed to be about equally ancient. All told—not of fixed habitation in these inhospitable lands, but of the exodus of some migrating tribe whose hunters must have travelled far with their dog sledges if the walrus and seal were as scarce then as now. No doubt the Arctic Highlanders who told Kane that an island rich in musk oxen lay far to the north, had occasionally despatched hunters in that direction; but no mere hunters would require such a town of huts, nor would they take the trouble to build on a new site at each visit without disturbing the circles of stone close beside them. Similar

ESKIMO REMAINS.

ancient remains have been found far westward through the Parry group, and have been attributed to that host which, in the fourteenth century, swept downwards from the unknown north and annihilated the Norsemen; but in our case the broken walrus and seal bones, though lichen-grown and evidently very old, could hardly have lasted five centuries even in an Arctic climate.

After three days' detention in Franklin and Pierce Bay, the ships succeeded in creeping up inshore past Cape Prescott and a broad glacier-headed bay, which has since been called after Professor Allman. Every one was on deck as we rounded Cape Hawkes into Dobbin Bay at midnight on the 12th August, for the scene that was opening beyond the tall shadow of the cape was one of unusual splendour, altogether different from such ideas of far Northern scenery as we had gleaned from books. It has somehow or other become conventional to represent Arctic skies as dark and lowering, and Arctic day as little better than uncertain twilight. Nothing could be wider from the mark, at least during the months that travel by ship and sledge is possible. Washington Irving Island threw a long shadow towards us across the lilac-tinted floes and gleaming water-spaces, which broke into ripples as our iron prow pushed towards them. As we rounded in close to the island, every telescope was fixed on a strange point on the top of the bluff standing out clear and sharp against the northern sunlight. It was either a very odd pinnacle of rock or a cairn, and that, too, remarkably well placed. We could soon decide, for the back of the bluff afforded a steep but practicable ascent. The conglomerate rock of the summit was smoothed off like a mosaic by the action of some ancient glacier, but near the edges it broke into a succession of rocky ledges, and on the topmost of these stood the object of our curiosity — a conical pile of well-packed stones. A second similar one stood a little lower down to the southwards, both plainly the work of a painstaking builder. But who was that builder? Not Eskimo. Structure and site forbade that suggestion. Civilised man had but once visited this shore, and that was when Dr. Hayes, in the spring of 1861, halted his tired dogs on the floes beside the island. He did not climb the bluff, and, besides, such an active sledge traveller would not have loitered to build a pair

CAPE HAWKS.

of cairns except at some crisis of his journey, and then he would have referred to them in his Journal. But the cairns themselves bore witness that they were not the work of any modern builder. Lichens grow but slowly in these regions. Dr. Scott found Sir Edward Parry's cairn untouched by them after thirty-two years, and the wheel tracks of his cart were fresh as yesterday's when, after the same interval, Sir Leopold M'Clintock crossed his track. These stones, on the other hand, were cemented together by deep patches of orange lichen—the growth of many generations. We found no record or scratched stone to tell us the names or fortunes of the men who had left the cairns as witnesses to us, their successors. Perhaps some baffled wanderer, whose fate is unknown to fame, had thus marked his furthest north. There is plenty of room for conjecture. Many have sailed for the northern Eldorado since Karlsefne, Celtic Norseman, left his Greenland home and launched his three ships on the first Arctic Expedition, eight hundred and seventy years ago.

For a week after leaving the island our progress northward was a constant struggle with the pack. Here, in the broad basin opposite Humboldt glacier, the Atlantic tidal wave through Baffin's Sea terminates, and leaves an icy barrier to mark its limits. Had not that barrier consisted of much broken floes lying off a continuous coast-line, it would have been impossible to force any ship through it; but, aided as we were by the shore, twenty-eight miles were made good in a week. Never did the prospects of the Expedition seem less cheering, but we comforted ourselves with the knowledge that the "Polaris," a fortnight later in the season, had made her magnificent run into Robeson Channel without much difficulty. With constant watchfulness and unremitting labour the way northward was won mile by mile. Every hour opened up some fresh possibility of advance, or some new danger to be combated. The tired watch-keepers found little rest during their short spell below. Almost every one "turned in" without undressing. The tearing and splintering of the ice along the ship's sides, and the creaking and crushing as she charged the floes, made sleep difficult. "All hands up screw and rudder," became a familiar order. And twice during the week it became necessary to cut docks in the floes to shelter the ships from pressure. On the first occasion, the heavy ice-saws, swung on tripods and worked by every hand on board, did their work readily; but on the second day they were found too short to reach through the thick ice, and nothing but rapid blasting with gunpowder saved the ships from an overwhelming crush. At length we found the rising tide flowing—not from the south as it had done, but from the unknown north. It was the 19th August. The barrier was

CAIRNS ON WASHINGTON IRVING ISLAND.

past. Pools and lanes of water became more frequent, and on the 21st we steamed through a sea which Morton, leader of Kane's northern party, might well call open, for the ice fragments floating in its intensely green water were not numerous enough to prevent a slight swell, which gave our wardroom lamps the old familiar swing.

As we pass Cape Constitution, Kane's furthest, the air, 6° below freezing, warns us that this year's navigable season is already far gone, but the dazzling sunlight ahead shows but little ice save the film already forming on the sea. Twenty hours' steam at this rate would take us beyond where ship had ever sailed. But, alas! "open seas" inside the Polar ice are disappointingly limited. Fragments of pack increase in masses, and at length stretch across the channel in a long white line from shore to shore. But a degree and a-half of latitude has been gained, and the 81° parallel lies five miles behind us as the ships are secured between Hannah Island and the grey cliffs of Bessels Bay. The island is merely a number of gravel mounds forming a convex breakwater in the entrance of the narrow fiord.

PLATE III.—MUSK OX HUNT, DISCOVERY HARBOUR, MIDNIGHT, AUGUST 25, 1875.

p. 25.

OUR first musk ox hunt led us to an isolated hill-top overlooking the bay in which H.M.S. "Discovery" afterwards wintered. This sketch was made on the following evening, from the spot where seven of the herd had fallen. Looking southward across the bay, and beyond Bellot Island, Lady Franklin Sound extends away to the south-west; and at the other side of the sound Grinnell Land rises in a line of straight cliffs, and spreads away towards Cape Leiber on the left, and to the distant peaks of the Victoria and Albert range on the right.

Looking northward from it, Hall's Basin lay before us, bounded on the right by Cape Morton and Joe Island, and far away beyond the mouth of Petermann Fiord the valley of Hall's Rest and the distant headlands of "Polaris" Promontory; while to the left, at the other side of the strait, the snowy cliffs of Grant Land formed the western lintel of Robeson Channel. There was little time to explore the island. A sketch which supplies the accompanying engraving was just complete when the signal

VIEW FROM THE TOP OF HANNAH ISLAND.

for recall flew from the foremast of H.M.S. "Alert." A lead had opened to the north-westward; the whole of the ice was in motion, and that night both ships reached the northern shores of Lady Franklin Straits before the closing pack barred further progress.

It was then midnight and very calm. A well-sheltered bay shut in by Bellot Island offered a secure harbour, and both ships entered it, steaming in towards a snow-covered valley at its head. Half-a-mile inland in the valley lay a cluster of dark objects; through our telescopes they looked like boulders; but as we watched them, wondering at their uniform size, they appeared to move. In a moment there could be no mistake. They were musk oxen, eleven of them in all, and within easy reach. A hunting party of six was soon organised, and in a few minutes a boat landed us on this yet untrodden shore. We separated in three directions, meaning to cut off the retreat of the animals landwards, but, unfortunately, our left wing engaged the enemy sooner than we expected, and they made off at a rolling gallop up a steep glen; two of them, evidently wounded, turned downwards towards a ravine to the left, but the main body vanished over the brow of a hill. So many pounds of good fresh meat could not be allowed to escape without an effort, and accordingly two of us started off up hill on the track of the game. They had made almost a complete circle, and we sighted them standing together on a steep isolated bluff nearly over where we had first seen them. Hidden by a projecting edge of the hill crest, we scrambled to the top up a slope of stones and snow, and surprised the beasts not ten yards off. They galloped right and left, heads down, and sweeping the snow with their long shaggy fur, but fell fast under the quick fire of our Winchester repeating rifles—murderous weapons for this sort of work. In less than a minute all seven were stretched on the snow.

It was now necessary to skin and cut up our victims, but before we commenced this very disagreeable duty, the reports of rifles in the valley below induced us to look over the brow. Our comrades had been reinforced by others from the ships, and a circle of assailants had closed round the wounded leader of the herd—a splendid bull. He was making his last stand close to the brink of a deep ravine, gallantly facing round at the flash of each rifle. He could no longer charge, but the angry toss of his head showed how dangerous it would be to close with him. He received no less than twenty-eight heavy Snider bullets before he fell.

Musk ox hunting is not, as a rule, exciting sport. The skinning and cleaning of the game, often in a cutting wind and low temperature, and the carrying of the meat on board the ship, involved a good deal of labour. Upon a subsequent occasion one of our hunters conceived the happy idea of making a wounded ox carry his own beef towards the ship, but the beast resented direction, refused even to be led by the horns, and finally overthrew his captor, and had to be despatched incontinently. They rarely attack, and can generally be approached within rifle range with little trouble. Sometimes, however, they are unaccountably timid. Animals that have never seen men are said to be devoid of fear; but our experience does not bear out the statement. Every beast we met, from the musk ox to the lemming, was afraid of us. They seemed to take some time to realise that we did not belong to their world. But having once made up their minds, they showed even more terror than wild animals usually do.

HEAD OF MUSK OX.

Each musk ox gave us about two hundred pounds of meat, often most excellent, but occasionally tainted with the flavour that gives them their name. We failed to ascertain the source of this characteristic. It occurs in both sexes and at all ages; and, moreover, it is not peculiar to the musk ox, for a haunch of reindeer presented to us by the Governor of Egedesminde possessed the very same flavour. A long course of preserved food makes most fresh meat acceptable; walrus and seal became delicacies; owls, foxes, and even skuas are not to be despised; but genuinely musky musk ox is fit for nothing more civilised than Eskimo dogs.

According to the programme drawn up for our Expedition before we left England, the second ship was not to be carried beyond the 82° parallel of north latitude. The sheltered harbour in which the ships now lay was 81° 41′, and was in every way suited for the winter quarters of our consort. Here, accordingly, the first stage of the Expedition terminated. So far everything we had hoped for had been accomplished. Depôts to cover retreat in case of disaster had been duly deposited at the Carey Islands and at Cape Hawkes, and a suitable harbour for H.M.S. "Discovery" had been found beyond Lady Franklin Strait, in a higher northern latitude than any human being had yet wintered in. Much of the navigable season still remained, and though we had all long ago realised the absurdity of expecting open water in the Far North, we could not but look hopefully forward to the long stretch of coast line shown on the charts extending to within 6° of the Pole, interrupted only by "Army Fiord" and " Navy Opening."

CHAPTER IV.

The Ships Part Company—Robeson Channel—Strange Ice—Lincoln Bay—A Gale—A Rush North—The "Alert" reaches a Latitude never before attained by Ship, and enters a Polar Sea—Precarious Position—Disappointment—No Land to the North—Perennial Ice—Altered Prospects—Autumn Sledging—Pioneering—Dog sledging—Romance and Reality.

N the 26th August the ships parted company, but the beginning of the voyage was ominous. A quarter of an hour after the "Alert" had received the last well-wishes of her consort, she grounded on a sunken rock, and got off again only to be checked within sight of her starting-point by a close-packed barrier of heavy floes. Two days afterwards she pushed successfully past Cape Murchison, but soon afterwards became entangled in a chaos of broken floes of most formidable proportions, and was forced to take refuge in a shallow bay with, fortunately, no worse injury than a broken rudder. While the rudder was being replaced, three more musk oxen were obtained, and, with our larder thus replenished, we entered Robeson Channel. Heavy floes completely filled the strait, moving rapidly north and south with each tide. Sometimes the whole pack would check for a moment against a projecting point of coast, and then rush on again, leaving a lane of eddying water filled with broken fragments between it and the wall-like cliffs. Through this lane, with a precipice of rock and ice-foot on the left, and square-sided floes gliding irresistibly past on the right, the path northward lay. It changed continually, one moment opening out invitingly, and the next closing like the jaws of a vice. It required the most unwearying watchfulness to advance through such a lead, especially as the numerous little bays which had so often enabled us to hold our own further south had now given place to an almost unindented coast. Late on the afternoon of the 27th we passed a broad inlet, which was identified as Lincoln Bay of the "Polaris." Twice we were forced back into its shelter. The second occasion was after an attempt had been made to force a passage through the pack away from shore. After an hour's charging and crushing amongst heavy blocks, the little patches of water became smaller and smaller, and the ship became beset amongst broken floes of most unusual proportions. The level surface of many of them was as high as the ship's sides out of water, and their whole thickness little if at all under eighty feet. The gentlest touch between such floes would be instant destruction; but, fortunately for us, there was much broken ice between them, and the ship was able to struggle away from the larger pieces till some change in the tide allowed her to escape back to the protecting land.

The first of September was an eventful day for the Expedition. A gale blew from the south-west, and after it had continued with undiminished violence for some hours, we could see through the drifting snow, blown in clouds from the land, that the ice was separating from the shore, and leaving a lane of water between it and the "ice-foot." Such a chance would not come twice, and there was no time to be lost. Under full steam, and with reefed topsails and foresail, our ship was soon flying northwards, trusting to chance for security when the floes would close again. Flying mists of snow left little to be seen but the black band of water ahead, and the bases of dark, steep cliffs on the left. We were passing Cape Union, but which of the numerous bold bluffs had received that name we could not tell. After a few hours, it was plain that it lay behind us, for the land began to trend to the westward. At noon the ship still advanced, but at right angles to her former course. The cliffs of Robeson Channel were past, and what could be seen of the shore was a low undulating beach fringed by a barrier reef of grounded icebergs. Our lane of water extended about two miles along this shore, and then ended at a low point of land, from which the pack had never moved in spite of the violence of the gale. The wind was now lessening rapidly, and the floes were closing steadily and resistlessly inwards. To be caught between them and the wall of grounded ice would be instant and hopeless destruction.

A mile behind us we had noticed a gap in the barrier of ice. There was just time to run back and push the ship through it, into the shallow water between the grounded ice-blocks and the shore, and to make her fast under the shelter of one of the blocks, when the pack closed in with a grinding crush that made some of us at least expect to see ice-barrier, ship, and all pushed high and dry on the beach.

In a few hours it again came on to blow, and this time furiously. The ice-pack was again driven off shore, carrying part of our barrier with it, the hawsers holding the ship to hillocks of grounded ice tightened like bars, and finally, in a fierce gust, snapt, and the ship drifted outside her shelter, but was again brought up by her anchor. Then the wind suddenly veered, and drove the ice in on us with alarming speed. There was no time to turn the ship; struggling sideways and sternwards through the tide of slush and tumbling ice that raced along the outside of the barrier, she reached the friendly gap just in time to be helped in by the closing pack. The roar of crushing ice had already commenced on the point of land north-west of the ship. It approached and increased every moment, till the whole beach was in full chorus, creaking, screaming, and crashing. Under such an enormous pressure the strongest ship that ever floated would have been reduced to matches in one minute.

For months afterwards the same harsh sound was to be heard outside our barrier, till it became familiar and commonplace. It can be very closely imitated by rubbing dinner plates together. As soon as the position of the ship ceased to claim immediate attention, many an anxious look was cast over the chaos of ice beyond in search of the coast-line to the northwards. The truth broke on us very slowly. President's Land was not there. The shore off which we lay curved to the left in a broad bay, and thirty or forty miles north-west of the ship the land ended in an abrupt cape. Behind us, and beyond Robeson Channel, Greenland spread away to the eastward, dwindling off in a perspective of rounded snow-covered hills, while to the north between these two lands' ends there was nothing but an icy horizon.

The whole sea was covered with floes varying from a few yards to miles in diameter. Their surfaces were undulating, and assumed peculiar blue and metallic greens in low sunlight. Small angular spaces between them were choked with fragments broken from the parent masses, and long irregular hedges made of similar *débris* surrounded each ice-field. These hedges rarely reflected the same tint as the floes; when one was purple, the other was green, and *vice versa*. It was months before we realised the full import of this ice. At first it seemed impossible that the great masses grounded along the shore could be mere fragments of sea ice we saw spread before us. We mistook them for icebergs. Like them, they were stratified. They grew in the same way, only the land is the parent of one, and the sea of the other. The Polar floes are in fact a floating glacier, and we accordingly called the fragments floebergs. In this the sea before us differed from ordinary frozen seas. Baffin's Bay, for example, renews its ice year by year. Every summer great part of it is, as we saw it, free from ice; in autumn,

PLATE IV.—FLOEBERG BEACH AND THE POLAR SEA, LOOKING NORTH FROM THE CREST OF CAPE RAWSON, JULY, 1876.—p. 29.

WHERE Robeson Channel opens out into the Polar Sea, the cliffs of Grant Land give place to a more shelving shore. This sketch, made late in July, 1876, and looking due north across the winter quarters of H.M.S. "Alert" at Floeberg Beach, shows the poleward prospect from the last of the cliffs. The coast-line curves away to the west into Black Cliff Bay, then turns north, and ends in the peaked mountains of Cape Joseph Henry, the point from which the northern sledge-parties started. Patches of melting snow, under Cairn Hill on the left, and under the slaty crest in the foreground (where some pink saxifrage is still in flower), send rivulets across the mud-flats to the South Ravine, and help to flood the green one-season ice between the grounded edge of the perennial pack and the shore. The floes are mapped out by hedges of hummocks, and look deceptively smooth from this height.

its surface freezes first into a pasty mass, then into floes nearly as flat as a frozen pond. During the winter, frost and snow thicken them, and wind piles them into hummocks. Sometimes part of the ice lasts for more than one year—thus whalers talk of ice of one or more seasons old. But the floes of the Polar Sea are perennial. They bear the plainest evidences of great age. They grow from above, and are stratified by seasonal deposits of snow slowly converted into ice. Excepting in insignificant spots along shore, the surface of the Polar Sea never freezes into new floe; it is never long enough exposed. The only ice of a single season possible here is a frozen together conglomerate of boulder blocks between the thick old floes. With this distinction in view, the term "Palæocrystic" was applied to this "sea of ancient ice." "Archaiocrystic" would more exactly represent what we meant, but sounds, if possible, more pedantic. The age of the floes is a subject for speculation; whether there is any limit to their thickness is also unknown. It does not in any way depend on crushing or piling together. They should be thinnest near land, where they are most frequently broken, and yet there were several on our beach—Floeberg Beach, as we called it—over eighty feet in thickness. We met with others floating so high out of water that they could not be less than two hundred feet deep. When strong winds and tides occur together during autumn, pools and fissures, crevasses rather, sometimes form in the edges of this polar-ice cap, but only those who have seen it can fully appreciate the utter impossibility of "boring" any ship through this polar pack; a nut-shell would have as much chance under a steam-hammer as a ship between the closing walls of such a crevasse. This was the open polar sea we had heard so much of, but which in truth no one in the Expedition had ever expected to sail in. What we had not calculated on was the absence of land northward; and that the coasts shown in the maps were absent was soon beyond all doubt. Day by day our disappointing position became plainer. The continuous coast-line upon which every hope depended was at least not in sight. One chance still remained. Possibly the land beyond Cape Joseph Henry turned to the northward, and though the ship had reached the utmost limit of navigation, sledges could travel along the frozen shore. Depôts pushed far northwards on a continuous coast-line would yet enable us to reach a high latitude, if that northward-running coast-line could be found at any reasonable distance from the ship. Meanwhile, it was plainly necessary to accommodate our aspirations to the stern negatives before us. The infinite possibilities of the unknown were no longer at our disposal. We could no longer cherish little unspoken hopes of rapid success, more navigable seas, richer hunting-grounds, or milder climate, polewards. Our ship lay about a hundred yards from the beach, her bows pointed to the north, her right side against the grounded ice which protected her, and on her left a space of shallow water stretching to the shore. Even this space was by no means "open water;" it was, on the contrary, filled with floating lumps of ice of every size, from that of a hailstone to that of a house, moving about with every change of tide. Some of the large ones were troublesome neighbours, and had to be secured with hawsers to prevent them getting into damaging positions. One of them, more erratic and less manageable than the rest, was commonly known as the Wandering Jew. The poet, by-the-bye, who placed that hero on a piece of polar pack, must have had a prophetic glimpse of these perennial floes ever drifting slowly round and round the pole. A few days after the gale the whole space between the ship and the shore froze hard, and it was possible to walk to land. The shelving beach was of rough shale, but, like the rest of the land, was almost entirely covered with snow. Much of the latter was soft and white, and had fallen recently; but here and there, in sheltered hollows, hard brown patches had evidently remained through the summer. Half-a-mile inshore low undulating hills rose to about four hundred feet. None of them had anything characteristic about them; they were simply rounded-off banks of brown slate and grey shale, with long straight slopes of hard snow on their northward faces—splendid places for headlong "toboggoning," as we found later on. Nothing could be more dismal than our new territory. But we still hoped that the next spring tides might allow the ship to advance a little way into some more favoured spot before she was finally frozen in for the winter. Two short excursions had already been made in search of safer quarters, but the reports they brought back were not encouraging. There were several bays not far north of the ship, but most of them were blocked with ice, which had evidently remained unmoved for many seasons. Under any circumstances, it was perfectly plain that the ship would be obliged to winter within a few miles of where she lay, and preliminary exploration of the coast westward, in preparation for the autumn sledging, could no longer be delayed. Accordingly, three dog-sledges were got ready to pioneer the road towards Cape Joseph Henry, to push forward a small depôt, and to search likely-looking spots for game.

Dog-sledges are to an Arctic Expedition what cavalry is to an army. They act as the feelers of the advancing force, do the scout work, carry despatches, keep up communications, and are in fact the Uhlans of a sledging campaign. Speed is their strong point, but in the long run dogs are unable to carry their provisions as far as men. They have, nevertheless, accomplished long journeys in latitudes where the pick and shovel had not to travel before the sledge, and where an occasional seal or bear helped out their provender. Looked at from a distance, there is a deal of romance about dog-sledging. Imagination immediately pictures the lively galloping team flying along over the crisp snow, and the comfortably muffled driver, covered with furs, reclining on the sledge, without a trace of baggage or provisions to inconvenience him. Alas! one half-hour's experience of the real thing is enough to take the whole gloss off the subject. The sledge is heavily laden with tent and sleeping-bags, provisions, and fuel—an item not considered by many people, without which even a drink of water is an impossibility. The driver toils along behind the sledge, guiding it by its handles as he would a plough, or flogging the dogs with all his might. Striding along in the deep snow gives him a peculiar waddling gait universal amongst the Eskimo. His companions run in front or behind, and keep up as best they can, painfully panting in the icy air, which sometimes brings blood from the lungs. When the sledge sticks in the snow, or falls into a crack, or jams between two lumps of ice, the dogs make one violent effort, and then stop doggedly till the sledge is lifted out for them. Then the driver hisses out "Kis, kis, kis," and the whip encourages any dogs that wont understand good Eskimo or forcible English, and off they go again. The Eskimo dog is, as a rule, utterly destitute of the ordinary virtues of his species. He is simply a wolf that has found slavery convenient. After the autumn sledging season, we tried hard to rear pups. Sometimes we got them large enough to toddle about the decks, and the fat little morsels would begin to answer to their names; but if we took our eyes off them for an instant, little "Samuel" or "William Henry" would suddenly disappear, and some near relative would look a little less hungry than before. When travelling, there is generally some unpopular individual in the team, and he is snapped at by all the rest. The dogs pull in the shape of a fan, constantly changing places, and thus tangling their tails in the traces. One elderly dog, appropriately called Bruin, had lost his tail in that way; some former Eskimo master had found it simpler to amputate than to unravel. More than once dogs were so severely bitten by their fellow-labourers that they had to be tied up in bread-bags, and carried on the sledge till they recovered a little. The meat biscuit provided for their diet was the only thing they would not eat. Hide sledge-lashings or whip-thongs were luxuries to them. One brute, called Michael, invariably ate his canvas harness, and upon one occasion ran off with the cook's metal ladle, and bit a large piece out of it. With all their faults, our dogs worked wonderfully hard. Their value to the Expedition can not be overrated. They could pull at a pinch nearly one hundred pounds each for a long day's march. Then when camping-time came, the driver whistled the signal to halt. A meal of preserved meat was served out to them, and they coiled themselves down in the snow, and slept with their bushy tails wrapped round their heads.

Most of our dog-sledging parties found it necessary to secure their teams during the hours called "night." This was done by detaching the united traces from the sledge, and fastening them to a spare

tent-pole pushed deep into the snow. Securing the dogs was not always a simple matter. Upon one occasion, the officer in charge had loosed the traces from the sledge for this purpose, when the dogs overpowered him, and started off at full speed across the floes, dragging him at their heels. He held on manfully, banging about like the tail of a kite; if he let go, good-bye to the team. Fortunately, the dogs divided on either side of an abrupt lump of ice, which checked them effectually, and put an end to his Mazeppa-like career.

A RAVINE IN THE STRATIFIED ICE.

CHAPTER V.

Exploration to the Westward—Dumb-bell Bay—A Seal—Search for Game—Lonely Lake—Fish in the Lake—A Gale—Return of the Boat Party—An Opportunity fortunately lost—The Expedition becomes *the most Northern*—Depôts sent forward—Frost-bite Range—Attempts to communicate with H.M.S. "Discovery"—Unexpected Difficulties—Soft Snow—Sunset—Preparations for Winter—The Snow Town—Building Snow Houses—Twilight Walk Shoreward.

N the 9th September, a party of four officers and four men, with three sledges, each drawn by eight dogs, left the ship for the westward to explore a route for subsequent crews, push forward a small depôt, and search the country for game. On the first day's march, our halt for lunch was ludicrously uncomfortable. A cold wind blew. All our water-bottles were hermetically sealed by the freezing in of the rough wooden plugs we had hastily fitted to them. There was nothing to drink but icy cold raw rum. One or two attempted it, and only succeeded in half-choking themselves, very much to the amusement of the rest.

When camping-time came, we found ourselves rounding into a narrow channel between two fine bays, whose "dumb-bell" shape at once suggested the title by which they were ever afterwards known. A strong tide in the narrow passage, representing the handle of a dumb-bell, had kept a small pool of water from freezing, leaving a hole about as large as a Trafalgar Square fountain. In this a seal was swimming about, turning his black shining head and large eyes from side to side in amazement at our appearance. All was fish that came to our net. He would at least make a good beginning for our game-bag. He was struck in the head, and consequently floated; but it was by no means a simple matter to get him out of the pool, for the ice was thin at the edges, and an unpleasantly swift-looking current was running below. Fred, our Eskimo, was equal to the occasion. Spread out flat on the ice, with a piece of cord in one hand and a batten in the other, he managed to reach the edge and secure our prize. He was rewarded for his exertions by a good share of liver for supper; indeed, no one at that time felt inclined to dispute the delicacy with him, for, by some mistake, our unpractised cook had fried a little of the blubber with it. The meat is very dark and rich, and is far from unpalatable; but if the least bit of blubber is cooked with it, it is exactly like mutton fried in cod-liver oil. This solitary "floe-rat" was the only seal shot in the Northern Sea. We had little sleep that night, the novelty of the circumstances, the low temperature of our beds, and the wind, which threatened to blow the tent over, kept most of us awake. The dogs too were behaving in an extraordinary manner. Something evidently made them uneasy; there was none of the usual snarling and growling going on. All at once there was a tremendous hubbub. We rushed out, and discovered that the brutes had scented out the spot where we had buried and *cached* our seal. They had succeeded in digging it up, and not a fragment was left. Fortunately, the skin and blubber were buried separately, and were still safe. Next morning our party subdivided. Three travelled forward with the sledges to deposit the depôt as far as possible northward and westward. Petersen, the Dane, experienced in snow-house building in Hayes' Expedition, set about constructing huts in a position that might be useful to later parties; and two of us started inland to search for game. The broad flats at the head of the bay looked promising, but were lifeless. Then we plodded on over the hills; not even a lemming track was to be seen. A few ridges were blown clear of snow, and sometimes the lee side of a red granite boulder would appear above the universal white. We worked towards a long westward-running depression in the land, hoping that there at least a little vegetation might exist; but on reaching the last ridge overlooking it, we discovered that it was filled with a sheet of green ice, stretching several miles to the westward. The lake—for lake it was—evidently discharged through gullies in the low hills at its farther end, and beyond these, twenty miles off, a range of pyramidal snowy peaks stood out clear and sharp against the calm green sky. When we stopped to secure a sketch, the lifeless stillness of our lonely lake was most impressive. No human eye had ever looked upon it before. And now there was neither bird or beast, or even tiny flower or blade of grass, to dispute possession.

About a mile from us on the left shore, a small rocky island caught a gleam of sunshine coming down through a ravine, and flickered strangely by refraction. The ice afforded easy walking towards it, but on reaching it we found that a rapidly-freshening wind was coming off the land, carrying clouds of snow with it, so that a retreat towards camp was plainly advisable. Before leaving, however, we set about piling up a few stones to record our visit. Under the edges of almost the first stone raised we were surprised to find the scattered vertebræ of a small fish. Some feathered summer visitor had evidently carried them there from the lake. We bottled the little bones in a small glass tube, and during two long days' most careful search for game, no other vestige or track of living creature was discovered.

Our return to camp was very near being enlivened by an incident. The wind had freshened so much, and carried such a quantity of large crystalled snow with it, that it was impossible to travel except in one direction—namely, straight before it. Fortunately, it blew directly towards our camp. So we started off across the lake, knee-deep or more in a flying drift which rustled like dead leaves in autumn. The ice was not thick even close to shore, for we had fired a bullet through it to try whether the water beneath was salt or not, and when we got about half-way across, it began to crack in an alarming manner, and to yield unmistakably to every footstep. We could neither stop nor turn back; the only thing to be done was to separate and shuffle on as fast as possible. The water soaked through cracks in our footsteps; but we were soon wading in the deeper snow of the land, and reached camp without further excitement, and thoroughly resolved to be more careful of untried ice in the future. Starting early next morning, we made a more extended, but equally fruitless, search for game. There was neither bird nor beast in the country, and but for a musk ox skull picked up near the shore we might have supposed that no living creature had ever visited the land. Punctual to their time, our sledges reappeared on the morning of the fourth day, having succeeded in depositing their load of pemmican on the further shore of Black Cliff Bay. The ice they had travelled over was so insecure in some places between the shore and the heavy floes that the sledges had broken through more than once, and the travellers had been wet through ever since they left us. There was evidently no game to be got, so we returned to the ship, and on the way back met a strong party hauling forward two boats in order to deposit them at an advanced point in readiness for the spring sledging.

Two days afterwards, on 14th September, a wind came from the south and gradually increased into a violent gale. The ice between the ship and the land broke up, and the pack again separated from the shore. The whole air was filled with drifting snow blown from the land, and flying past in a dense cloud higher than the topmasts. It was only in the lulls that it was possible to distinguish the shore not one hundred yards off. The boat party had not yet returned, and we were not a little anxious about it; but late in the evening a figure was seen signalling from the beach. A double-manned boat pushed off from the ship, and, after a tough struggle, pulling in the teeth of the gale, reached the shore. Then we learnt that the returning crews had narrowly escaped being carried off by the breaking-up ice, and were about two miles from the ship dragging an exhausted man on the sledge, and thoroughly fatigued by their long forced march against the gale. Assistance was promptly despatched to them; all were soon brought safely on board. The severity of the weather was not the only reason why we were anxious that the sledge parties should be on board. A crisis in our fortunes was approaching, for the pack was still moving from the shore, and in a few hours it might be possible to advance the ship a little further westward, and perhaps a mile or two further northward. As the drifting snow became less thick, and the weather cleared, we saw that the opportunity had come. Once more we heard the joyful order to get up steam. The rudder was rapidly got into its place, but no efforts could get the screw into its bearings. The fresh surface water entangled about it froze when it was lowered into the colder salt sea beneath, and while all hands were still working at it, the pack closed in as tightly as before. We were all greatly disappointed at the time, but there is now not the slightest doubt that if H.M.S. "Alert" had advanced two miles to the westward she would never have carried her crew southward again. It was from henceforth evident that the ship would have to winter in the spot where chance had placed her, and every effort was at once directed to the sledging.

There was no time to be lost; winter was fast approaching; day and night had again returned. The sun's dip below the icy horizon to the north was longer and longer every night, and during the day he skirted so low above the southern land that even at noon it was already dusk in our wardroom and between decks. Light fleecy snow fell frequently, and day by day the temperature declined nearer and nearer to zero; but nevertheless, no change took place in the outside pack—it still roared and grated in constant motion. The idea of travelling over it could not be entertained for a moment, and it was necessary to wait till the snow of the shores and the new ice of the inlets and narrow spaces between the pack and shore were hard enough to bear the loaded sledges. On 22nd September the dog-sledges again started for the north to ascertain whether Cape Joseph Henry could be crossed or rounded. And two days later, three eight-man sledges, under Commander Markham, with Lieutenants Parr and May, left the ship with a heavy load of provisions and stores, to be deposited at the most northern suitable fixed point in readiness for the spring campaign. Lieutenant Aldrich and his dog-sledges returned in fourteen days. He had reached the Cape, crossing on his way the ring of latitude from which Sir Edward Parry, the most poleward of our predecessors, had turned back 48 years before. From a cliff two thousand feet above the polar floes, he had seen nothing but ice to the northward; but far westward, seventy miles or more distant, snowy headlands, one beyond the other, extended slightly northward of the land on which he stood.

This was the worst news we had anticipated. It left the future undecided. If his telescope had detected the loom of land to the north, our duty would have been plain, and success at least probable. If, on the other hand, the coast beyond the Cape ran definitely south, the clear negative would have allowed us to turn every energy into a new channel. But now this new-found land must be tracked westward for many a weary mile, and those distant headlands must be rounded one by one before we could be certain that the coast-line did not finally turn polewards, and afford a route which might be followed, if not next year, at least in the following season.

Wind, insecure ice, and constant falls of snow told heavily against Captain Markham's three sledges, but they successfully deposited their depôt near the Cape, and in such a position that anyone travelling along the beach could not fail to find it even in fog or storm. On their way back, part of the ice they had recently sledged over was found destroyed by the motion of the pack, and it was necessary to haul the sledges over the summits of the Black Cliffs. There, there was no shelter from the wind; the temperature fell to 47 degrees below freezing. That bleak ridge was afterwards known as "Frost-bite Range." When, after three weeks' absence, they reached the ship, the whole party was in a wretched condition. Their sleeping-bags, robes, and tent were stiffened into boards of ice, more than twice as heavy as when they set out; and the twenty-four men and officers had no less than forty-three frost-bites amongst them, most of them comparatively slight, but three so severe as to require amputation. While these sledge parties were laying out the autumn depôts and exploring northward, others were no less active in another direction.

The programme of our Expedition stipulated that the "Alert," in order to keep up communication with her consort, was not to winter more than two hundred miles from her. An officer and sledge crew belonging to the "Discovery" had accompanied us northwards with the intention of returning to their ship as soon as the "Alert" had reached her winter quarters. We had advanced but sixty miles, and yet the most gallant and persevering efforts to communicate with the "Discovery" were again and again unsuccessful. The deep soft snow lying piled against the cliffs of Cape Rawson and Black Cape barred the way. The men, buried to their waists in the snow, dug a path for the sledge till the excavation became a tunnel, and a day's hard labour could be measured by a few paces. The last and most determined effort to force a road southward was undertaken on the 2nd October, but on the 12th the party returned without having got further than six miles from the ship. This failure to communicate with the "Discovery" over so short a distance as only 60 miles was altogether unlooked for, and could not but suggest uncomfortable reflections. It had been assumed that even two hundred miles would not interrupt communication between our ships, and that sledges could travel the whole length of Smith's Sound to reach a relief ship, or to deposit despatches at its entrance. Where was the error in the assumption? Were our men degenerate? Our picked crews, full of health and strength, and enthusiastic to a man, were equal to the best of their predecessors. The conclusion was inevitable—the conditions and not the men were to blame. Within half-a-mile of our ship, there were many places that would stop the finest crew that ever drew a sledge. The ice was massive beyond all expectation; but it was not the ice that stopped our travellers—it was the soft snow. Some idea of its fleecy lightness may be gathered from the fact that ten measures of it could easily be pressed into one, and that one melted into only one-tenth its bulk of water. Everyone noticed the beauty of its crystals; they were delicate eighteen-rayed stars, rayed not in one plane, but in all. In British Columbia and other parts of Canada, when such soft snow interferes with travelling, it is usual to camp for a day or so—perhaps under a comfortable tree—and, when the snow has hardened a little, make a firm path for the sledge, or long tobbogin, by tramping in advance on snow-shoes. But we might have waited till permanent darkness set in before our snow hardened. Our sledges, perfect as they were for their own work, were not suited for land travelling over soft snow; and as snow-shoes had never been used by Arctic Expeditions, we had but two pairs in the ship. There are two causes that tend to harden and cake the surface of snow—the first is wind, and we had comparatively little of that; the second is a contrast in temperature between the earth below and the air above the snow. When the lower part of the snow is twenty or thirty degrees warmer than the upper, evaporation takes place from the one, and condensation in the other. At Floeberg Beach the earth was permanently cold. Even in midsummer only a few inches of the surface thawed, and during the whole winter it remained close to zero, so that it was not until the intensely cold weather of spring that any marked contrast was established.

Two days before the return of the last autumn party the sun sank below the south horizon, not to return for nearly five months. We climbed Cairn Hill to have a last look at him, but the high land southwards hid him from view. His refracted rays still lit up the ice of the northern horizon, but Floeberg Beach and the pack, for a mile outside the ship, lay in the shadow of the land. Away southwards to the right, the sides of the Greenland hills caught the sunlight, and through

INSIDE THE SNOW HOUSE.

the gaps in their undulating outline a distant horizontal plain of *mer de glace*, the northern termination of Greenland's continental ice, was yet distinguishable at intervals.

After the return of the depôt detachment from Cape Joseph Henry, the twilight had darkened so much that further sledging was impossible, and all hands set about making preparations to encounter the fast closing-in winter. Firm ice had formed round the ship, and cemented her to the grounded floebergs on her right; but, in order to guard against being again blown from shore, she was secured to the beach by two strong chain cables, supported at intervals by barrels, so that the heavy metal links should not sink into the ice. The "crow's nest" and all the rigging that could be spared were taken down from aloft and packed away. A thick felty awning was spread overhead across spars fastened between the masts so as to completely roof in the greater part of the ship. Then snow was heaped up all round her black hull as high as the crimson stripe along her bulwarks. But for her masts and yards she might have been taken for a great marquee, with stove-pipes coming through at intervals. Her unshipped rudder was hung across the stern,

PLATE V.—WINTER QUARTERS *OUTSIDE*, FROM THE FLOES ASTERN OF H.M.S. "ALERT," DECEMBER, 1876.—p. 37.

DURING winter moonlight this view of the ship was a familiar one; for it is from the end of the half-mile marked out for exercise on the floes. The foretopmast has gone to make a roof-tree for the thick awnings that house in the deck. The crow's nest and much of the rigging are packed away till next wanted. The unshipped rudder hangs across the stern, out of the way of damage from any crushing of the floes. Snow packed up carefully all round the ship is an all-important protection against the increasing cold.

safe from any ice pressure during the winter. To enter the ship, one had to pass through a narrow gap in the snow embankment, near the middle of her left side, ascend two or three steps, and lift up a hanging door closing an entrance cut in the bulwarks. The whole of the upper deck was covered with a deep layer of snow, so as to keep the heat in. Snow passages, with double wooden doors, self-closing by means of weights, were made over the two hatch-ways leading down below. The skylights were all covered up. Lamps and candles had already been in use for some time. By means of eight stoves, distributed in various parts between decks, and each burning twenty-eight pounds of coal per day, an average temperature of forty-nine was maintained through the winter. It was intended to utilise all the heat by leading the flues along the deck overhead before they passed up into the outer air; but the horizontal flues smoked so much that it was necessary to let them pass directly upwards, and even then they were as smoky as ships' stoves usually are. Meantime, the bleak beach opposite the ship was also undergoing metamorphosis. Boats, spars, blocks of patent fuel, casks, and cans of stores innumerable had been carried to it from the ship, so as to increase the habitable space on board. The casks and barrels were piled into walls, and roofed in with spars and sails, so as to make a large storehouse to hold everything that could be taken from the ship. A short distance off, a great pyramid of pemmican, stearine-fuel, bacon, and other sledging stores rose above the snow. Next came the preparations for the scientific observations of the winter. The wooden observatory, on a firm foundation of snow-filled casks, looked like a bathing-box unaccountably gone astray. Then a whole group of beehive-shaped snow-houses, each one the temple of some special instrument, the "Declinometer," the "Unifiler," and so on, and a whole system of catacomb-like passages cut in the deep snow and roofed in, connected the buildings.

Fortunately, the last gale had so far hardened the snow-drifts in this spot that snow-house building had become possible. Every few days a new "house" sprang up. A group of men would come out from the ship, warmly booted and mitted, carrying shovels and saws, and perhaps a lantern. They shovel off the loose surface snow, and proceed to mark out two sets of concentric circles, one slightly larger than the other, and follow the marks with the saw driven vertically into the snow. The rings thus sawn out are then cut into blocks about two feet square. The outer ring of blocks from the larger circles, placed round the circular pit left by the removal of blocks from the smaller set, makes the first tier. Then comes the outer ring from the smaller set, and so on alternately, till a good flat block closes in the top. The resulting edifice is all in steps, but it is thoroughly substantial, and will last till midsummer. Thus our town sprang up, and each part soon received its appropriate name—Markham Hall, Kew, Deptford, Greenwich, &c., while at a safe distance southward an eccentric edifice, surmounted by a broom handle to represent a lightning conductor, acted as magazine and spirit-store.

Long before winter had passed, our town had disappeared as completely as Nineveh or Pompeii. Only an uncertain mound here and there projected over the bleak slope of drifted snow. Some of the storehouses, indeed, were so effectively hidden that they were not found till after several days' excavations in the following July. The great advantage of a snow-house is that it takes its temperature from the earth, and not from the air. Some of ours were occasionally as much as forty degrees warmer than the atmosphere, so that an observer well muffled in furs could remain for four or five hours at a time watching the swinging magnetic needle, or the progress of some icy experiment. His meditations would sometimes be disturbed by the wandering footfall of one of our dogs overhead, sounding strangely loud and reverberating. The snow was curiously retentive of odours: a little spirit spilt in one house made it ever afterwards smell like a gin-palace; another had an unaccountable odour of oysters that puzzled all our *savans*; but, as a rule, the smell of burnt candle predominated. The manner, by-the-bye, in which the flame of a candle gradually sank into a tallowy net-work cylinder afforded a striking illustration of the still air and low temperature of a snow-house. In strong moonlight, or after daylight returned, the effect inside one of our buildings was most peculiar. The snow transmits a subdued greenish-blue light, such as a diver sees deep under water.

While twilight lasted, many excursions were made landwards, but the uncertain state of the deep snow made even a short walk a serious undertaking. In places it lay merely dusted over the ground; in others in deep drifts, here soft, and there hardened by wind. If we turned to the north, we soon came to a steep ravine, by no means easily crossed, winding down from Mount Pullen. All inland was a monotonous waste of snow, and ten minutes' walk to the south brought us to another ravine—a smaller one—which somehow or other acquired the name of the "Gap of Dunloe." Here a summer torrent had cut a way under the ice and snow that half filled the ravine. A few

BUILDING SNOW-HOUSES.

little frozen pools amongst the boulders was all that remained of the torrent, but its size might be estimated by the long flat cavern it had washed out under the ice, lit from above by a number of dangerous "man-holes" opening through the snow overhead. At the other side of the ravine, the land rose towards the high capes overlooking Robeson Channel, and afforded very rough walking, for the vertical slate strata was either smoothed over with treacherous snow, or stuck up through it in various-sized flat slabs, making the land look like a vast graveyard. As a rule, however, there was really nothing to see but interminable snow. Sometimes, when it was a little overcast, even the distinction between land and sky was confused, and everything assumed a uniform whiteness. More than once it occurred to us that our scenery was very simply portrayed: a spotless sheet of white paper could not be improved upon. Under such circumstances, it may easily be imagined that the discovery of a hare track was quite an exciting event. Who could think of returning to a half-past two o'clock dinner before the track was followed, and the quarry found! A second hare track was fallen in with on the 29th October, but after following it for some hours it became plain that the creature had more than once been within thirty yards, and had escaped unnoticed in the twilight. The chase was given up, and it was at any rate a satisfaction to know that at least one live thing was left to pass the winter in our neighbourhood. There was no use in trying to hunt after this. That day we had hoped to get something better than hare, for one of the ice quartermasters had reported that he had heard wolves howling inland during the middle watch, and wolves would hardly pay us a visit so far north unless they were driving musk oxen or reindeer. A long walk on snow-shoes failed to discover any tracks, and indeed the beasts themselves might have been close at hand without being seen, for darkness was already stealing over the land.

EFFECT OF EXTREME COLD ON A CANDLE.

CHAPTER VI.

End of Twilight—Moonlight—Daily Life in Winter Quarters—Condensation—Breakfast—Morning Prayers—Outdoor Work—Exercise—The Ladies' Mile—A Walk to Flagstaff Point—Sounds from the Pack—Optical Phenomenon—Dinner—Our Cat "Pops"—Occupation during Winter—Mock Moons—"Sally"—The Darkness.

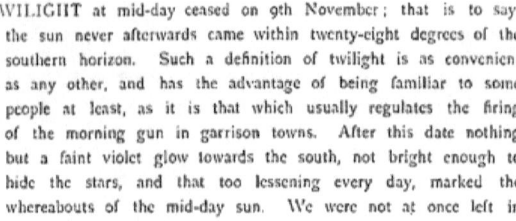

TWILIGHT at mid-day ceased on 9th November; that is to say, the sun never afterwards came within twenty-eight degrees of the southern horizon. Such a definition of twilight is as convenient as any other, and has the advantage of being familiar to some people at least, as it is that which usually regulates the firing of the morning gun in garrison towns. After this date nothing but a faint violet glow towards the south, not bright enough to hide the stars, and that too lessening every day, marked the whereabouts of the mid-day sun. We were not at once left in darkness, however, for the moon rose, and for ten periods of twenty-four hours—one cannot call them days—climbed, and then declined spirally through the heavens. She again visited us three times before twilight returned, each time giving us the benefit of full moon; indeed, without her cheerful visits winter darkness would have been almost unendurable. During the intervening periods of darkness, "next moonlight" was looked forward to in much the same way that schoolboys look forward to holidays. A diagram made by Captain Nares, and hung up on the lower deck, representing the daily position of the moon during the absence of the sun, was constantly consulted. In this far northern region man is as much influenced by the moon as his celebrated Ascidian ancestor on the tidal beach. Her advent inaugurates a period of intermittent vitality. Then was the time to build snow-houses, to collect fresh ice for culinary purposes, and to repair the banking up of the ship. It was only then that it was possible to leave the beaten track marked out for daily exercise, and wade towards Cairn Hill or Flagstaff Point, or toboggin down Thermometer Hill or Guy Fawkes Hummock. When the moon left us, exercise collapsed into a monotonous two hours' routine up and down, up and down the measured line of preserved meat tins, relieved here and there by an empty barrel, by way of milestone. A tread-mill would have been a pleasing exchange, especially if it was made the means of supplying an electric light during exercise hours.

Anyone acquainted with Arctic literature does not need to be told that a polar winter cannot be safely passed without strict discipline. Routine must extend even to the smallest domestic affairs. Some people would never go to bed, and others would never get up if there was nothing special to make them; and constant darkness is so enervating that few, if any, would keep up a steady healthful amount of exercise without routine.

Let us take a single day as an example of life in winter quarters. On waking in the morning one's first sensation is that there is a chilly spot somewhere amongst the blankets. A drip of condensation from the cold deck overhead has found its way through the waterproof or rug

PLATE VI.—THE DECK: MORNING INSPECTION AND PRAYERS.—p. 41.

MORNING muster and prayers on deck formed part of the daily routine, and, while the long darkness lasted, every day began with this scene. The men are clad in seal-skin and cork-soled carpet boots. The deck is covered in with a deep layer of snow, and snow-houses are built over each hatchway.

spread like a canopy to intercept it. This condensation is one of the greatest nuisances we have to contend with. Its chief sources are our breath, evaporation from damp clothes, and culinary operations, but there are many others. All the oil used in our lamps, and every candle we burn, is converted into nearly its own weight of water, and must condense somewhere. It either falls in large drops, well coloured with candle and lamp smoke, or reserves itself for warmer weather by freezing in all the nooks and crannies overhead and at our side. A little press close to the bed holds our summer boots, a number of glass instruments for chemical experiments, and some spare candles; but we have just discovered that the whole set of articles are imbedded in a solid block of ice formed by repeated condensation. An odour of kindling coal floats into the cabin as the wardroom stove is lit, and warns us that it is time to get up. Some minutes elapse before the chilled flue will draw, hence the odour. Toilet is not a lengthy operation. A tub is a weekly luxury, for water means fuel. The men have already breakfasted, and are clearing up the decks. The plates, cups, and saucers are cheerfully rattling on our mess table, and our next-door neighbour kindly warns us not to be late, as curried sardine day has come round again. A large mess-tin of cocoa is simmering on top of the stove, and the baker has treated us to the unusual luxury of hot rolls. At ten o'clock the men muster round the tub of lime-juice, mixed with warm water, and each man's name is marked off as he drinks his allowance. Then all hands parade on deck for inspection. Everyone is dressed alike, in yellow sealskin cap and coat, sealskin or duffle trousers; long carpet boots with thick cork soles keep the feet well off the snow, and are especially comfortable over two pair of lambs'-wool socks and a pair of fur slippers. When the officers have inspected their detachments and reported all mustered, the chaplain reads the collect for the day and a brief prayer by the light of an engine-room oil-lamp hung from overhead. All join in the familiar responses, and the beautiful words of the prayer for the navy sound more than ever applicable to our special circumstances. The scene is a striking one. The dim yellow light, the composed fur-clad men, the awning draped in feathery pendants of ice, and the trampled snow on deck, make a picture not easily forgotten (Plate No. 6). Immediately after prayers, all hands are told off to the work of the day. The declinometer house is closed up with a snow-drift, and has to be dug out. Ice has to be dug out with picks from the top of a floeberg, and drawn on a sledge on board to be melted for drinking, cooking, and washing. The water thus obtained is only too pure. Frozen sea water, in spite of theory, remains salt, but the upper strata of the floebergs are pure snow condensed into ice. Then there are some stores to be drawn on the strong working sledge from Markham Hall; and the blacksmith and his assistants have a number of shovels to repair, for, strong as they are, they wont stand levering out blocks for snow-houses. At one o'clock the men go to their dinner, and before ours there is yet an hour and a quarter. We cannot stay on board, for the wardroom is occupied by an energetic party rehearsing for theatricals. We have just time for a good smart walk. In a few minutes we are equipped, with long mitts—some people call them elbow-bags—slung round the neck, and a substantial muffler tied sash-wise over one shoulder as a reserve in case of necessity. On first going into the open air, there is a faint odour like that of green walnuts. It is difficult to say what is the cause of it; it is not always noticeable, and does not coincide with the darkest staining of the ozone tests. The measured half-mile is already full of figures tramping along, some singly, some in pairs, some fast, others slowly, but all keeping to the beaten track, for elsewhere the snow is soft and the ice is hillocky.

Let us, for sake of variety, take advantage of the waning December moon, and visit Flagstaff Point. It is only a mile and a-half northwards, but the deep snow will keep us beyond our time unless we wear snow-shoes. The sloping shore hills are barred with "sastrugi"—wind-made ridges of snow—but the abrupt scooped-out rifts between them are smoothed over with fleecy powder in gentle undulations like the swell of a sea. The crests of the snow waves are often marked with long sinuous lines of black dust blown from uncovered spots. A short alpenstock is useful to feel the way. We carry no arms, for we are beyond the region of the sea bear. The fierce creature depicted on our crockery (p. 83) is altogether out of place; but then every one supposed when we left England that the far north was chiefly characterised by abundance of bears, brilliant aurorae, icebergs, and Eskimo. The point is marked by four barrels supporting a flagstaff. Beyond it lies a seemingly level plain, between a wall of pack-ice and the mouth of our north ravine. The temperature is 67° below freezing; but it is perfectly calm, and not too cold to rest for a moment or two.

RETURN FROM A WINTER WALK.

In this icy wilderness there is an overpowering sense of solitude, which adds greatly to the weird effect of moonlight on the floebergs, fantastically-shaped and vague. There is complete silence, but it is broken every now and then by sudden unearthly yells and shrieks from the still moving pack, harsh and loud as a steam siren, but unlike anything else in art or nature. As we return to the ship our attention is caught by a brilliant star, so close to the rough and indistinct horizon that it looks as if some one was carrying a lantern on the floes. As we watch it, it moves, at first but a little, but afterwards in long curves like the sweep of a goshawk. It took us some time to find out that the motion was an optical delusion, most distinct when no other stars were near.

The cheery sound of the first dinner gong has brought every one in off the ice; and as we enter the ship, we find a group of our messmates brushing each other down with a housemaid's brush, for one must be careful not to carry any snow into the warmth below. A lantern lights the way into a snow-hall built over the hatchway. We open the inner door, a rush of cold air precedes us down the ladder, and we descend in a cloud of vapour like an Olympian deity. For a moment the changed atmosphere and a suspicion of tobacco smoke makes us cough, and the glare of lanterns and lamps dazzles. There must be no delay in taking off our sealskins; they are already moist with condensation, and a cold steam streams from them to the floor. Little lumps of ice on the eyelashes and brows soon melt, but a solid mass cementing beard and moustache together resists even warm water for a time. Hair about the mouth is a nuisance in the Arctic regions, and everyone keeps close cropped. Our vice-president's two sharp taps on the table announce grace; he will wait for no one when the soup is cooling, and quite right too. Our dinner is the same as the men's: a piece of salt meat left from yesterday *rechauffé*, preserved meat—there is a discussion whether the pie is mutton or beef—preserved potatoes, and preserved onions; we shall have carrots to-morrow. Lime juice replaces beer, for the latter has become a rare luxury, reserved for birthdays and other state occasions. Presently some one throws a good conversational fly; if it is very successful, a brisk controversy follows. The subject is immaterial, all are more or less exhausted, and none is proscribed except theology. It is wonderful how many subjects became theological before the end of the winter. We have laid in a small stock of wine, which allows us to have two glasses of sherry or Madeira with dinner. When that is disposed of, conversation flags, and the table is soon cleared. As soon as the cloth, which looks as if it had been used before, is removed, our white cat springs upon the table, and seats herself in the centre with all the assurance of a spoiled pet. It is not a little strange that both she and "Ginger," her sister, forward in the men's quarters, as well as the Eskimo dogs, and even "Nellie," the black retriever, suffered from epileptiform fits. Before winter was over, Pops got so strangely feeble that she could not spring upon a chair without several efforts; but when summer came, and we got her a little fresh meat, she recovered perfectly, and returned with us in safety to England. After dinner was a quiet time to write up journal, to read, or to work at some experiment or observation. Certain instruments had to be registered every hour, and sometimes even every ten minutes, day and night, and fair registers of such observations occupy not a little time. One or two who have work to do at night put in a couple of hours' comfortable sleep before tea is announced at six o'clock. Then follows school on the lower deck. When it is over, and the officers have dismissed their pupils, the musician of our mess, whose good fellowship is equal to his skill, treats us to a little of his exhaustless fund of music. Strange to say, our piano still keeps excellent tune in spite of the heavy seas that swept the wardroom crossing the Atlantic, and many a severe freezing since. A game of chess, or a rubber in the captain's cabin, concludes the evening.

We were all prepared for a long and monotonous winter, and each one, according to his proclivities, had drawn out for himself a lengthy programme of improving study. One would read through Alison's "History of Europe," another would master Italian, a third preferred German; others chose music, and would learn the banjo, or, if the mess preferred it, the tambourine. But the historic programme only was carried out. Most of us found that our time was more than occupied with notes and observations of Arctic Nature that we might never have another opportunity of making. There was the electric, magnetic, microscopic, thermal, and chemical states of earth, air, ice, and water, and a hundred other pressing questions, that made us regret we had not spent our whole lives in preparation for our unlimited opportunities. Then there was other work that could not be postponed.

It was above all things necessary to ascertain the exact position of our winter quarters, so that the geographical discoveries of the Expedition—the coast-lines passed by the ship as well as those traversed by sledges—might be fastened down to at least one fixed point. For this purpose, many careful observations of moon and stars were required, and the officer who had accepted the duties of astronomer had no easy time of it. He and his assistant spent many a chill hour watching the occultation or transit of some star or planet. The observatory is necessarily open to the air; snow-wreaths festoon its walls and corners. Every breath freezes on the metal and glasses of the telescope; even the vapour from the observer's eye quickly clouds the lens. His assistant, utterly unrecognisable under a pile of furs and mufflers, stands shivering beside him, carefully keeping a chronometer from the cold, for neither watch nor chronometer will work in the temperature of Arctic night.

The weather during winter was, as a rule, so calm and clear that observations on the stars could be made almost at any time; but it was not a little remarkable that, even at the clearest times, some icy dust, too fine to be called snow, was always falling. On the 27th December, for example, it was so clear that a star of the third magnitude less than three degrees from the northern horizon could be satisfactorily observed. And yet, in twelve hours, a glass plate exposed on top of a neighbouring hill collected a quantity of little crystals equal to nine tons per square mile. These crystals, not to be confounded with icy dew formed on the plate itself, were altogether too small to be seen with the naked eye; but there was no difficulty in using a microscope, even in the lowest temperatures, except that the mercurial reflector was soon destroyed by the cold. It was when these crystals assumed their simpler shapes, and were abundant in the air, that the moon appeared decked in those halos and crosses known as *paraselena*, or mock moons. Twice in December we had good examples of them. Upon each occasion the moon appeared in the centre of a large and luminous cross, surrounded by two circles plainly distinguishable between us and the snow-clad land. The cross swayed and trembled with every breath of air, and vanished altogether when wind disturbed the tissue of falling crystals; but the halos were more permanent. Plate No. 7 gives a better idea of them than any verbal description. It is a reproduction of a sketch made early in the morning of the 11th of December. Our long-lost wanderer, Sally, absent since 15th October, when she was left by a sledging party near Sickle Point, had just put in an appearance, and may be seen in the foreground intensely watching the proceedings of two officers engaged in measuring the holes with a sextant.

A propos of Sally, her adventures might make a canine romance. She was a young, rather unsociable, grey-coloured Eskimo dog, that formed one of Lieutenant Aldrich's team in his autumn sledge-journey into the "untrodden north" and past Cape Joseph Henry. Like several others, the cold and hard work were too much for her, and she broke down utterly. The more "fits" she had, and the feebler she got, the more she was set upon and bitten by the stronger ones. It was impossible to delay the sledge, and there was nothing to be done but either shoot the poor beast, like a canine comrade a few days before, or adopt a less merciful course and leave her on the floes, with a faint hope that she might revive and limp home after the sledge. It was late in September that Sall was thus cast adrift. On 22nd of October the men of Captain Markham's party fell in with her, still lingering about the spot where she had been abandoned, very lean and hungry, but too wild or too feeble to follow them back to the ship. From that time she was written down in the roll call as "expended."

Week after week of cold and storm and darkness passed, and everyone felt quite certain that poor Sall had gone to the happy hunting-grounds. It is accordingly easy to imagine that

PLATE VII.—WINTER QUARTERS *INSIDE* H.M.S. "ALERT"—THE WARDROOM.

THE warmth and comfort inside the ship were a strong contrast to the chill loneliness outside. In the snug lamplight of the wardroom, with a journal to be written up, or a book from the well-stocked shelves behind the door, it was easy to forget that only a few planks and a bank of snow shut out a thousand miles of darkness and deadly cold.

her reappearance on 11th December caused a decided sensation. Even her old comrades could not believe their eyes, but growled and stared at the gaunt prodigal that sat wolf-like on a snow hillock, and howled dismally in the moonlight. Ever afterwards she was a changed dog. She grew large and strong, and her character became ambitious and overbearing. When she set her mind upon anything, she got it, whether it was an empty box to sleep in, or a neighbour's pup for supper. She became the favourite of the "king dog" of the pack (dogs soon learn, and never forget which is master), and would feed between his paws. But after a while she learnt to beat her lord, and finally usurped his throne, and led the pack in work or play, though Salic law is generally observed amongst Eskimo dogs. When the Expedition returned, she was given to our trusty Eskimo Fred, who knew how to value her. Some of us would have liked to have shown her in England, but it would have gone hard with the first cab horse she caught sight of.

The "Alert" in her winter quarters at Floeberg Beach was 142 days without the sun—a week longer than the "Polaris," and a month longer than any previous English expedition. Throughout the whole time the difference between noon and midnight was hardly appreciable, but a long period of slowly lessening twilight preceded actual night. Our darkest time occurred between moon-set on 18th December, 1875, and moon-rise on 4th January, 1876, though indeed the periods preceding and following it were scarcely lighter. Many a time, as we stumbled blindly along at daily exercise, we discussed the question whether our noon was really as dark as an English moonless night. The general impression was that it was not so dark. The universal snow husbanded what little light there was, and sometimes looked almost as if it was self-luminous. Although the sun was further off on the 23rd December, that was not the darkest day, for the moon was not far below the horizon. That day at noon it was just possible to count lines 3 millimetres wide when not more than 4 millimetres apart.

The 28th was perhaps our darkest day. In order to retain some idea of what the darkness was, we took a rough "Letts's Diary" out on the floe at noon, and tried to read the advertisements printed in large type at the end. It was necessary to remain out some ten or fifteen minutes in order to get accustomed to the darkness; and of course, if one had any idea of what the advertisements were beforehand, the test did not apply. The words "Epps's Cocoa," in type nearly half-an-inch long, were easily read, but the "breakfast" in small type between them was utterly illegible. It was just possible to spell out "Oetzmann" in clear Roman type five-sixteenths of an inch long; and after much staring at the page, held close before the eyes, we managed to make out "great novelty" in type one-fourth of an inch long. Of course the test depended as much upon the eyes as upon the darkness; but it was at any rate a comparative one which would enable those who tried it to recall the darkness of their winter noon.

The line below will give an idea of the size of type

LEGIBLE AT MID-DAY.

We have since found that such type is legible on clear moonless nights in England.

CHAPTER VII.

Winter Climate—Preservative Effect of Cold—Falling Temperature—Unprecedented Cold—Extreme Low Temperature not Unendurable—A Visitor from the Shore—Cold : Vitality—Sudden Changes—A Breeze from the South—Warm Wind Aloft—Danger from East Wind—Dawn—Brilliant Effect of Low Sunlight—Lessening—Sunrise—Preparations for Spring—Snow-shoes—Our Prospects—Motion of the Floes—A Tide Wave.

AS the absence of the sun lengthened, so the cold increased. Arctic Expeditions have almost invariably registered their lowest temperatures in February and March, the months in which the earth is coldest even in England. The darkness and the low temperature of winter do not occur together: the cold, indeed, belongs rather to spring than to winter. In our case, it was not till after darkness had left us and dawn was well advanced that the state of our thermometer became a subject of general interest.

We did not expect an unusually cold winter. Maps marked the "pole of cold" far south of our position, and it seemed likely that the great polar sea, though much the reverse of open, would make our winter warm. The thermometer stands were conspicuous objects as we came out from the ship to the floes. The first was supported on a barrel and snow pedestal only seventeen feet from the ship, so as to be convenient for hourly or half-hourly registration. Then came the self-registering thermometer, elevated on a tripod about thirty yards from the ship. Others were placed on the floe near shore, and on a hillock close to the beach.

It may be said to be always freezing in the far north. Even in a warm summer day, when the air is perhaps 40° Fahrenheit, flakes of ice rise up from the cold sides of the floebergs, and in the shade float in a thin pellicle on the water in the ice-cracks. Meat exposed to the air keeps all the year round, and for many months our rigging was decorated with sides of musk ox and carcases of mutton. In connection with the keeping of meat, it is worth while to mention that a piece of musk ox meat, exposed for six months in the rigging, and sealed up in the cold air, remained, very unexpectedly, unchanged when the temperature rose, and was exhibited perfectly fresh three months after the Expedition returned to England.

The temperature of the air sank permanently below freezing in the middle of August before we had reached winter quarters, and continued below for nine months. Fifty-four degrees of frost were registered during the October sledging. In November, mercury froze and the spirit thermometers fell to forty-five below zero (*i.e.*, 77° of frost). The lowest in December was one degree colder. Then hopes of a warm winter were given up, and we watched the spirit shrink degree after degree past the coldest recorded by our predecessors. January's lowest was 58°.7; February brought 66°.3 below zero; but on the third of March, three days after sunrise, the unparalleled temperature of 73.7 degrees below zero was indicated by our Kew-corrected thermometers, and for many hours the temperature remained more than one hundred degrees below freezing.

INTENSE COLD.

As a general rule, people look upon extreme cold as the most characteristic and most insupportable part of Arctic service, but this is altogether a mistake. It is not nearly as trying as the long darkness, and both are insignificant compared to the social friction of the confined life— a friction which would be unbearable if the men and officers had not been accustomed to habits of discipline, and inured to the confinement and restraints of "man-of-war" life. The hardships of mere low temperature are by no means unendurable. In comfortable winter quarters, and with plenty of dry warm clothing, we found the extremest cold rather curious and interesting than painful or dangerous. An icy tub on an English winter morning feels colder to the skin than the calm Arctic air. Cold alone never interrupted daily exercise. It was possible to walk for two or three hours over our snow-clad hills, in a temperature of one hundred degrees below

freezing, without getting a single frost-bite, or perceptibly lowering the temperature of the body. It is possible even to perspire if one works hard enough. The fact is, only the face and lungs are really exposed, and neither appear to suffer from it. Our experience led us to think that men, thoroughly prepared, might safely encounter far lower temperatures. Many a time, as we sat round the stove on the main-deck discussing the events of the day and the state of the weather, the relative merits of Arctic cold and tropic heat were warmly canvassed. Several of both our officers and men had lately returned from the Ashantee campaign, and they could speak with authority. There was one thing clear—one could sometimes get warm in the Arctic, but never get cool on the Coast.

If the intense cold was more endurable in winter quarters than some of us had anticipated, it was altogether a different thing camping out away from the ship on a sledge party. Then, with food and clothing limited by the sledge-weights, with no warmer bed than a snowdrift, and no possibility of changing ice-saturated clothes, cold, far less than that experienced in winter quarters, becomes a real hardship, and its miseries can hardly be exaggerated.

During the period of intense cold, we amused ourselves with many experiments on its effects on various substances. Ordinary spirit, such as brandy or rum, froze into crystalline paste. Even the alcohol in our astronomer's spirit levels acted sluggishly. Glycerine became as hard as soap; mercury remained frozen for ten or twelve days at a time. Everyone knows the danger of handling metal at low temperatures. The danger depends greatly upon the state of the hand; if it is at all moist or soft, it will adhere, and soon be dangerously frostbitten; but if quite dry, we could, for experiment sake, take a mitt off and turn the brass handle of our outer door without experiencing anything more serious than a sudden sting, which was like neither heat nor cold. It was even possible to melt a small fragment of mercury on the naked palm without leaving a trace of injury.

We had few opportunities of noting how the lower animals bore the cold. Our Eskimo dogs evidently suffered much at times, but never learnt to use a snow-kennel built to shelter them. Some of the bitches had sumptuous apartments constructed for them on deck, in the vain hope that comfort would make them more careful of their offspring. One old dog, Master Bruin, who had no tail to coil round his neck when he went to sleep, and was perhaps more susceptible to cold on that account, discovered that the magnetic observatory was warmer than the star-lit side of a hummock, and would willingly have taken up his quarters there if it had been allowed. Nellie, the retriever, always took her daily exercise, but slept between decks in the warmth. Pussy paid one visit to the deck just to see what Arctic winter was like; but she hopped about shaking one foot after another, and sneezed so incessantly that she seemed in danger of choking, and had to be taken below again.

Neither rats nor mice had come north with us. Three of our useless carrier pigeons had reached winter quarters alive, fluttering round the ship and perching on the frozen rigging, but none survived long. It was in the depth of winter, when the land seemed utterly lifeless and deserted, that the first living inhabitant of Floeberg Beach presented himself on board our ship. Midnight was past, and one officer alone lingered beside the main-deck stove, watching the red light flickering on a much-weathered musk ox skull that had been picked up on shore and was now being dried before the fire. Suddenly he falls on his knees and stares intently at the bone, then rushes to the naturalist's cabin, and reappears with that gentleman lightly clad in scarlet flannel, and bearing the first bottles and specimen boxes that came to hand. A little black spider, revived by the warmth, had crept out of a small hole in the skull, but retreated again before he could be bottled. Two weary hours elapsed ere he reappeared, but the watchers were at length rewarded, and he was triumphantly captured, packed away, dated, and labelled in the naturalist's store, commonly known as "South Kensington."

At that time we had an unreasoning impression that no live thing could endure actual reduction to the temperatures of Arctic night. But cold is by no means so deadly. The mosquitoes, butterflies, and dragon-flies of brief Arctic summer are assuredly not all new arrivals. A good example of vitality in the vegetable kingdom was afforded by the wheat left at "Hall's Rest" by the ill-fated "Polaris." In spite of the cold of five winters, it was still alive when we found it. Sown at Discovery Bay, it germinated freely, and, as I write, some of it carried home with the ships promises to reproduce itself in a fair crop of bearded "Polaris wheat." Even at the Polar Sea, and in

PLATE VIII.—LUNAR HALOES.—p. 44.

THIS is a sketch, from the floes alongside the ship, of an unusually distinct Paraselena that appeared on 11th December, 1875. The haloes and cross round the moon are caused by the passage of her light through a tissue of impalpably minute needle-like crystals of ice slowly falling through the atmosphere. The snow-covered hills of Floeberg Beach are in the background, and in the foreground two officers are measuring the arc with a sextant, while the long-lost Sally looks on. In summer the sun was often surrounded by a similar meteor, but intensely dazzling, and tinted with colours like an outside rainbow.

PLATE IX.—THE DAWN OF 1876. H.M.S. "ALERT" IN WINTER QUARTERS.—p. 49.

DAWN in the latitude of Floeberg Beach is a season rather than an hour, and the growing brightness skirts round the whole horizon almost impartially. This is a sketch very early in March, looking north at midnight. At the time it was made, the spirit thermometers on the small stand, and on the tripod seen to the left of the ship, registered -70° Fahrenheit. The outlines were made without much difficulty, with a pencil pushed through two pairs of worsted mitts. The colours were laid on in the warmth and candle-light between decks, and verified by repeated trips into the cold. In regions where wind could crush the ice together, or where open water existed to leeward, Arctic ships have more than once been blown to sea with the ice of their winter quarters; and, as a precautionary measure, our ship was secured to shore by chain cables, raised at intervals on casks to prevent them sinking into the ice.

the midnight of winter, the air holds spores of moulds, and many of them grew rapidly when carried into the warmth inside the ship. It is hard to say what temperatures would kill such primitive organisms—in fact, so far as our little experience goes, Sir William Thomson's "moss-grown fragment of another world" might have carried the germ of terrestrial life safely enough through the chills of stellar space.

The temperature of winter was by no means steady; on the contrary, its progressive fall was interrupted by many sudden rises.

In ordinary cold weather the sky was wonderfully clear, and the weather wonderfully calm. Many a time, as we walked at daily exercise up and down our half-mile of shadowy snow, with nothing to look at but the stars, the whole sky was absolutely vapourless, from the pole star in the zenith to Orion or the three stars of Aquila just skirting along the horizon. Sometimes a faint fleecy mist, hardly distinguishable from one of our feeble auroras, would pass overhead; but round piled-up masses of cloud, such as are common in southern skies, were never seen.

A change rarely came unexpectedly. Often for days beforehand "mare's tail" clouds, with a hard wavy outline, would float up against the faint moonlight in the southern sky, and spread themselves into wings and fingers over Robeson Channel. Then, with a sudden gust from the south, and a mist of flying snow from the land, the temperature would rise. Mercurial thermometers would thaw, and soon register as faithfully as spirit instruments beside them. After a while the wind begins to come more and more from the westward. The thermometers remain high, but the wind feels piercingly cold wherever it can find a way inside our sealskins. While the storm lasts, it is impossible to go outside the ship. Whirling snow hides everything. Even on deck exercise is uncomfortable, for powdery snow floats in through every chink in the carefully-closed tent-like awnings. Notes on the instruments on shore have to be suspended, for no one could force a way as far as the beach through the darkness and whirlwind of drifting snow; and if they could, they would find the observatories so buried that it would take several hours to dig out their doorways. Even the thermometers within seventeen feet of the ship were not always easily registered. Upon one occasion the officer in charge of the meteorological work had to confess himself beaten, after two determined attempts to reach and register them. In twenty-four hours or more the storm lessens, and gradually dies away to a gentle breeze from the northward; and with it the temperature declines, until it is as cold or colder than before.

A striking change of this sort came in December. From thirty-five degrees below zero, the thermometers rose rapidly with a gusty southerly wind till the temperature reached the freezing-point. This strangely warm wind cannot have travelled far in contact with the frozen earth, for it was being rapidly cooled. The quick changes, with every puff of wind, suggested the advisability of trying what the temperature was in the air overhead, and it was discovered that the higher we climbed up the rigging the warmer it got. The main-top was three degrees warmer than the deck at the same instant, and a thermometer secured high aloft in the cross-trees actually registered + 36°—a temperature which can hardly be accounted for by supposing that the wind was warmed by passing over pools of open water in Robeson Channel or Smith's Sound.

At times, when the air was undergoing rapid changes of this sort, it was striking to find that, by boring a hole into the ice with an auger, it was possible to get down past zero, and reach the temperature of yesterday or last week before coming to + 28°·3, the steady temperature of the Polar Sea beneath.

Although such warm southerly breezes sometimes occurred, our winter was on the whole marvellously calm. During its earlier months, the wind was anxiously watched. Our safety depended entirely upon its direction. A north-easterly wind might force the whole polar pack with irresistible pressure upon our unprotected shore. Many parts of the beach bore witness to the effects of such pressure in former seasons. Vast blocks of ice, thousands of tons in weight, had been forced high upon the shore, pushing up redans of mud, sand, and shells before them. It was not pleasant to contemplate the enormous force which had accomplished such work, and might any day repeat it. And our autumn efforts to reach the "Discovery" gave us poor encouragement for a march southward from a crushed or stranded ship.

Towards the end of January a pale violet light made its appearance over the southern horizon. It was at first only noticeable at noon, and the glow was so faint that stars shone brilliantly through it. It heralded the returning sun, and every one watched it hopefully. It and the increasing cold were the two staple subjects for every conversation. Day by day the faint noon-light imperceptibly increased, till, in the first week in February, a tender greenish glow succeeded the violet, and for an hour at noon we could fairly call it twilight.

If any part of Arctic life deserves the sentiment and romance that have been lavished on it, it is returning daylight. However practical and matter-of-fact a man may be, a long spell of Egyptian darkness will make him glad to see daylight again, and he may well be excused a little unnecessary emotion at the dawn of the pale young year. With us the day and the year were all but the same. When daylight was once established there was no more real night, though the sun made thirty-seven more and more shallow dips below the horizon before rising spirally through the heavens in perpetual day. Winter was our night, and the morning and the evening were spring and autumn. As February advanced, we began to have light enough to walk about on shore. Up to this time we had laboured under two disadvantages that had not oppressed our predecessors—namely, the extra noon darkness and the softness of the snow. Both together rendered it utterly impossible to indulge in exercise except along the well-trodden half-mile, with empty meat tins for guide posts, or backwards and forwards to the shore along the track of the sledges carrying stores to and from "Markham Hall." It was not till we were able to walk about a little at noon that we got impatient of the dark-ness, and began to realise its length and intensity. The transition from darkness to daylight was like recovery from a long and somewhat delirious illness.

As the light increased, the sky displayed all the colours of the rainbow, from rosy red at the horizon to cold violet overhead, and the ice, borrowing the spectrum sky tints, assumed hues of indes-cribable delicacy and beauty. A few hundred yards ahead of the ship some acres of floe had stranded and split into bergs with narrow lanes between them. The cliff-like walls afforded convenient sections of the ice, where its varying saltness and its strange lines of "air dust" could be favourably examined. Accordingly, these narrow clefts were well explored, and in them especially the low light produced most magical changes of opaline colour. Such effects are unsketchable. Form there was none, but while the low light lasted the tints of the ice vista were incredible—a brilliant transformation scene would look commonplace and natural beside them.

Our walks were not carried very far from the ship before we discovered that other animals had begun, like ourselves, to take advantage of the returning daylight. Even while the darkness was at its greatest, men carrying lanterns to and from the water-berg or the shore occasionally noticed the little lines of curved scratches left by lemming. What the little creatures could have been doing out on the floes we could not understand; their tracks usually led into deep cracks and fissures of the ice. Perhaps they found warmer quarters near the water. After daylight one could hardly walk half-a-mile on shore without coming across their burrows—little circular tunnels leading long distances under the snow, either to saxifrage pastures, or to warm nests made of grass that must have taken them a long time to collect. Sometimes we came across them sitting near their burrows. They were about the size of a small rat, almost tailless, and as yet in their yellowish white winter fur. Later on, ermine tracks were met with, but they were much less common. They were generally found pursuing lemming, but upon one occasion it was quite plain that the ermine had followed a hare. Of course whoever met a hare track was bound to follow it. Three hares remained in our neighbourhood; they lived in burrows in the snow five or six feet long; two were shot, but the third would never allow us within rifle range.

On 29th February the sun rose, but those who climbed to Cairn Hill to see him were disappointed. The high flat land southwards shut him from view. On the 2nd of March, however, when we mustered as usual by sledge crews on the floes beside the ship, bright sunlight lit up the tops of the higher floebergs and shone on the upper parts of the ship's rigging. The Greenland mountains were already pink, and as the sun approached the gap between them and Cape Rawson, half his orb was seen for a moment by a few who climbed the rigging to look for it; the others thought they could well wait another day after waiting so long.

The month after sunrise was a busy time for all hands, for there was much to be done before the whole strength of the Expedition was diverted to the sledging campaign.

Although there was broad daylight outside the ship, the work inside had still to be done by lamp and candle-light. In one place a group of figures might be seen surrounded by open packing-cases, carefully weighing out sledging-rations, and dividing the daily allowances in little bags made of fancy calico intended for theatrical purposes; in another an officer and the captain of his sledge might be seen filling a large gutta-percha box with the stores to be placed in depôt for his return journey. Everywhere through the ship men were busy with needle and thread making many small improvements in the fit of their duffle suits or holland overalls; some were adding linen leggings to their mocassins, others strengthening the soles with thick soft leather cut from the top of their fishermen's boots. The general sledging outfit was of course rigorously adhered to, but each man made such small changes in the fit of his clothes as his autumn experience suggested.

During the darkness the snow had hardened considerably; in many places a sledge now travelled readily where it would have sunk out of sight in the autumn, and as early as the 28th February an exercise party travelling with a dog-sledge to the south reached in a few hours the spot from which our autumn sledges had returned baffled after a ten days' struggle towards the "Discovery."

But the snow was not hardened everywhere. There were many drifts and patches along the shore that were not easily crossed except on snow-shoes. With these, travelling over smooth snow was easy, and a man could even pull along another seated on a small sledge, faster than a third could wade beside them. No Arctic expedition had hitherto used snow-shoes, though the Germans three hundred miles south of us on the east coast of Greenland had found it necessary to extemporise rough substitutes during the winter. Some of our men made two excellent copies of a well-worn pair presented by Dr. Rae to one of our officers. These were at times most useful, but much of our travelling was over snow and ice so rugged that no one, however expert, would have attempted snow-shoeing.

Constant preparation for the sledging soon superseded the winter evening routine. School was suspended, and the theatrical season closed on 24th February with a very successful burlesque written by our chaplain. On the following Thursday the weekly lectures were concluded by an address from the captain on the sledging work we were about to undertake, and on the prospects that lay before us. Those prospects were not promising, however we looked at them; they were no more encouraging than when we first rounded Cape Rawson and saw no land to the northwards. The very first elements of success were absent, but it was still possible that the land might trend to the north somewhere beyond Cape Joseph Henry. It was possible, too, that sledges journeying northward over the floes might reach some land where depôts could be left, and which might next year serve as a fresh base for poleward sledges.

A few in the ship cherished a third hope, founded on the character of our ice. It seemed not unlikely that if sledges could penetrate that zone of the floating ice-cap which had been fractured year after year by contact with the shores, they might reach a broad mass of almost continental ice rounded into hills and valleys by ages of summers, but not offering insuperable obstacles to poleward travel.

If the floes had not been in rapid motion all the autumn, and if Sir Leopold M'Clintock's method of pushing forward sledges on depôts deposited in the autumn could have been applied to the polar pack, we might start from the land with fair hopes of practical success. But, as it was, our sledges would have to leave shore carrying *all* their fuel and provisions, and therefore greatly limited in point of time, for no men can drag more than between forty and fifty days' provisions and fuel, together with tent, bedding, cooking-gear, and sledge. The system of supporting sledges was still applicable. By it additional sledges would fall back from the main party when say one-third of their provisions were expended, retaining a third to return on, and filling up the advancing sledges with the remainder.

We were by no means certain that the motion of the floes would not even now prove a serious obstacle. Even as late as January they were heard roaring and crushing in the darkness to seaward, and their pressure forced our protecting floeberg somewhat shorewards, cracking and buckling up the floes, and heeling the ship over four degrees. For months, however, little sign of motion had been apparent except at tidal periods, when it sometimes came with curious suddenness, as if the tide wave had all at once overcome the resistance of the ice that bound it. For example, the morning of the 12th of March was beautifully calm and still, and few but those whose special duty it was knew that a high tide was due that day. I was engaged picking out some stones grooved and scratched by ice-motion from an overturned "floeberg" not far from the ship, when suddenly a curious faint sound came from the north-west, at first a dull, indistinct hum, but in a moment it grew nearer and louder, like the rush of a railway train. Then, as it swept down along the beach, the ice cracked visibly in every direction with a sharp rattle like musketry, and a loud rush of water under the floes came so suddenly and unexpectedly that I ran to the top of the berg with a vague idea that the ice was breaking up. But in a moment the tide wave had passed off to the south-west, and all was still again.

PLATE X.—THE "ALERT" IN WINTER QUARTERS, FROM AMONGST THE BARRIER BERGS, MARCH, 1876.—p. 50.

NOWHERE is it more true that "the low sun makes the colour" than in the Arctic regions. The ice and snow, that are wearily white in midsummer, glow with all sorts of opaline tints in the sunrise light of March. The sketch is from amongst the floebergs to seaward of the ship. The sides of the berg in the centre have been worn into columns and alcoves by the surface floods of some former summer; but it has since been forced higher on the beach, and into shallower water. Snow-drifts fill up all the gorges and ravines amongst the bergs, and are in some places so hardened by wind and infiltration of sea-water, that tidal motion cracks and fissures them, especially round the grounded bergs.

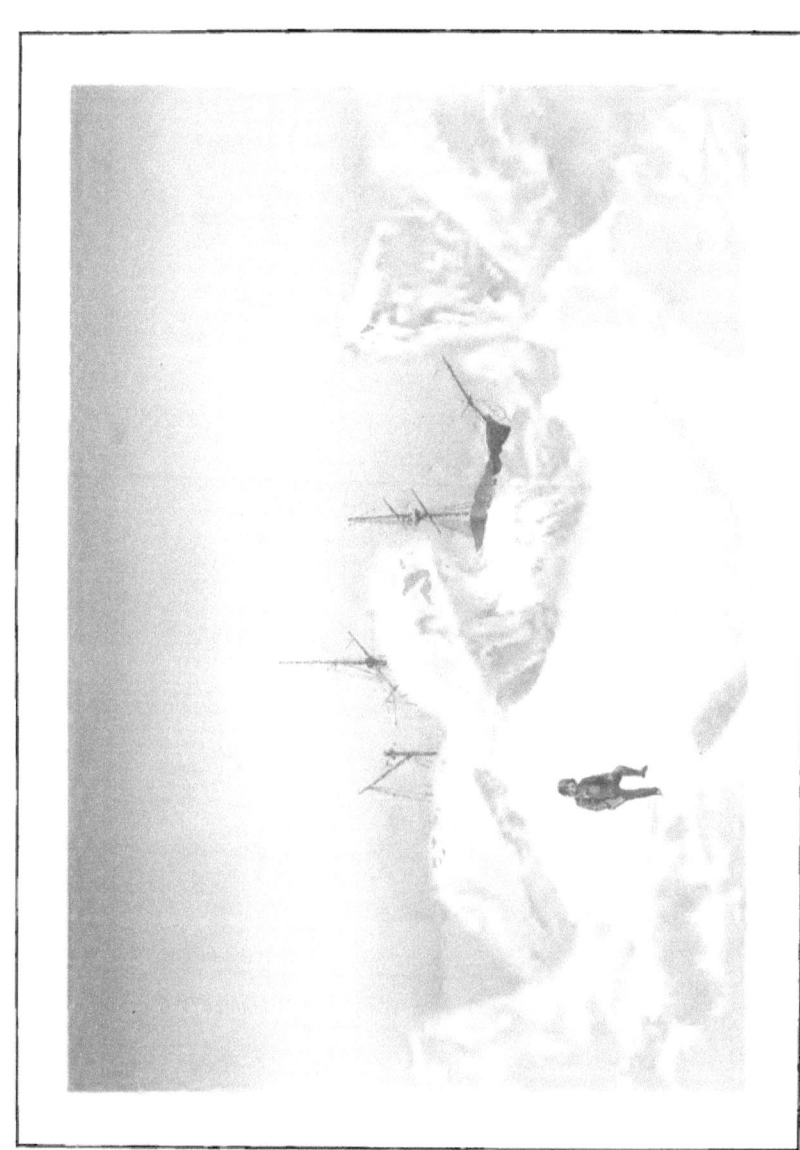

CHAPTER VIII.

The Sledging Campaign Opens—A Push for the "Discovery"—Petersen Breaks Down—Shelter in a Snowdrift—Difficulties in Retreat—A List of April Cases—Programme of Spring Sledging—Limited Hopes—Departure of Main Detachments—Double Banking—The Camp—A Night in a Tent—A Typical Floeberg—The Hare's Sanctuary—Coat of Arms—Castle Floe—Parhelia—Road-finding in the Fog—Mirage—A Crevasse.

THE failure to communicate with H.M.S. "Discovery" in the autumn had to some extent disarranged our plans. Communication was absolutely necessary to ensure co-operation, and the sooner it was effected the better, for our consort had as much sledging work to get through as she could possibly complete in the season.

Robeson Channel had to be crossed, and the rugged northern shore of Greenland explored in search of land poleward. Peterman's Fiord had not yet been traversed, and Lady Franklin Sound might possibly open northwards, and afford a favourable route for the "Discovery's" sledge-crews to penetrate as far as the shore of the Polar Sea.

The short travelling season in the far north is limited on the one hand by the lingering cold of winter, and on the other by the summer thaw of the surface snow and the renewed motion of the ice. As soon, therefore, as travelling was at all possible, a dog sledge was got ready to carry despatches to our sister ship. Two energetic young officers and Niel Petersen the Dane were detailed for this duty. On the morning of 12th March everyone in the ship gathered on the floes to see them off. Their team of nine dogs carried the "Clements Markham" down the smooth ice of our exercise mile at a gallop, and in a few minutes the red and white sledge pennant with its crossed arrows was lost to sight amongst the hummocks off Cape Rawson.

Three days passed in preparing the ship for spring, and the low temperature and strong wind made us think anxiously of our absent messmates, but we never for a moment supposed that they would suffer anything more than the recognised hardships of sledging in bad weather.

On the evening of the third day, our heavy winter awning had just been taken down from over the deck, and the men were coming inboard after their day's work, when some one caught sight of the dog sledge coming back to the ship. There were but two men running alongside, and they came on silently, without the usual joyful signalling that marks a returning party. Poor Petersen lay on the sledge, marvellously changed in three days, mottled with frost-bite, and apparently dying. His companions had succeeded in carrying him back to the ship only just in time. They themselves were much fatigued, and their fingers raw with frost-bites incurred in attempts to restore Petersen's frozen limbs. When they had slept, as only tired men can, we heard their story.

They had not been a day away when Petersen found he had greatly overrated his strength, and became unable to assist in the heavy work of guiding the sledge along the steep incline under the cliffs, lowering the dogs and sledge down precipitous places, and hauling them up again. Next day he was badly frost-bitten, for a cramped and enfeebled man cannot long resist strong wind and a temperature of minus 34°. It was impossible either to proceed or retreat without risking his life, and the breeze freshened, so that they could not pitch the tent. The only course left was to dig a pit in the snow, which was, fortunately, somewhat hardened by the wind. So they at once set about shovelling out a hole, and when it was six feet deep they excavated it below till they got a space eight feet square. It took six hours' hard labour before they were able to move Petersen, wrapped up in the tent and tent robes, into it, and cover the top closely in with the sledge and drifting snow. But once well covered in, and the sledge lamp lit, they had the satisfaction of seeing the temperature rise to 7° above zero. But Petersen could not be warmed. They made tea for him—he could not take it; pemmican disagreed with him; and a little soup was made from the Australian meat carried for the dogs. By turns they chafed his limbs for hours at a time, and thawed his frozen feet under their own clothes, Eskimo fashion, then swathed feet and hands in their flannel wrappers, and lay close on either side trying to warm him; but in a very short time, although he said his feet were warm and comfortable, they were found frozen so hard that the toes could not be bent, and the whole process had to be gone through again. For a day and a night they struggled in this way against the fatal cold, and then, fortunately for them, the wind lessened, and leaving provisions and fuel, dogs' food, and all that could be dispensed with, behind, they took the only course open to them, and struck out for the ship. The only possible road was the one they had come, and it was rugged in the extreme. On the left rose high cliffs banked with treacherous snow, and on the right rounded and broken ice piled in towers and pinnacles upon the shore. In some places round headlands it was utterly impossible to get the sledge safely past with the man and tent robes lashed on it, and one had to help him round as best he could, while the other held in the eager dogs and tried to guide the sledge. The poor brutes were so anxious to get back to the ship that constant halts were necessary to disentangle their harness, no easy task with frost-bitten fingers. The last headland was the worst. In spite of every effort the sledge slipped sideways, then upset, and rolled down into a deep ditch, turning over three times as it went, and dragging the dogs after it. When it was at length got out, a comparatively smooth road lay before them, and they drew up alongside the ship, most thankful that their comrade was still able to recognise the friends that crowded round him. For days the poor fellow lay in a very uncertain state. Severe amputations were unavoidable, but he rallied wonderfully for a time, and when the main detachments of sledges left the ship we bade him a hopeful good-bye.

Five days passed before the weather became calm enough for a second attempt southward, but on the 20th the dog-sledge again started for the "Discovery." The settled weather that favoured our travellers this time, enabled us to take active measures to prepare our sledge crews for their coming work. Each day a pair of crews left the ship for practice with their sledges, and thus a store of pemmican, bacon, &c., was deposited at Black Cape to help forward the Greenland division of sledges from the "Discovery."

Before breakfast on 1st of April a man came down with a report that a large white animal had just been seen a quarter of a mile from the ship. This seemed a very extraordinary piece of news, for our walking parties had scoured the whole country, sometimes as much as thirteen hours away from the ship, without finding even a track of game, and had as yet brought nothing on board except one small white feather from the breast of a ptarmigan or snowy owl.

The general opinion at first sight was that the date added a peculiar significance to the story, but at any rate it was advisable to lose no time in seeing whether the mysterious animal was sufficiently "materialised" to leave any tracks. Accordingly two of us took our rifles, and sure enough we found a large wolf track at the spot indicated. For hours we patiently followed the marks. They took us a long circuit shoreward. There appeared to be three animals, but we could not be certain, for the track often doubled on itself. All at once an unpleasant suspicion flashed across us—could it be that anything had happened to our travellers, and that we were following their dogs in mistake for wolves? The tracks were very large, measuring as much as six inches long by four and a-half wide, and the centre nails were long, and turned outwards. While we debated, our suspicions were set at rest by a loud howl, not as prolonged as a black Canadian wolf's, but wolfish certainly, for there was no mistaking the fierce misery of the note. He had caught sight of us, and, as usual with his species, given a view halloo. Presently we saw him, three hundred yards off—a gaunt, yellowish white beast—cantering along at a swift slouching gait. When we stopped, he stopped. We lay down, and one of us rolled off on the snow out of sight, and made a long detour in hope of surprising him, but he seemed to know the range of our rifles to a nicety, and at length we saw him canter off southwards unharmed by the long shots we sent after him. As we walked back, we could not but wonder what had induced wolves to come north into a desert where for miles and miles there was not so much as a stone above the snow. The mystery was soon explained. Tracks of four hunted musk oxen were found a couple of miles off. No doubt the wolves had driven them from some southern feeding-ground. They travelled so rapidly that our hunting party despatched after them failed even to catch sight of them.

The discovery that there was some game in the country was a very cheering one. If it was not a land flowing with milk and honey, it was at any rate not so bad as it might be, and we went back to our sledging preparations with a hope that we should fall in with either the wolves or the oxen during our travels.

The weather was now sufficiently settled to warrant the departure of the main travelling parties. It was arranged that they should consist of two separate divisions of eight-men sledges. Lieutenant Aldrich, with the sledge "Challenger," would explore the shore to the north-west in search of land trending northward. He would be supported by Lieutenant Giffard's sledge, the "Poppie," which would travel with the "Challenger" to a distant point, re-provision her there, return to Floeberg Beach, and then carry out depôts of food and fuel for the "Challenger's" homeward journey.

The northern division, under the command of Captain Markham, would consist of his sledge, the "Marco Polo," and Lieutenant Parr's, the "Victoria," supported by the "Alexandra," commanded by Mr. White, and the writer's own sledge, the "Bulldog." In addition to these, a four-man sledge led by Briant, a petty officer of H.M.S. "Discovery," would help us forward for three or four days. The routes of both detachments lay together as far as Cape Joseph Henry. At that point the northern parties would replenish their stores from the supporting sledges and from the large depôt of pemmican placed there in the autumn, then, leaving the land, endeavour to force a passage due northward over the floes. Meantime, a depôt for their return would be carried out by the "Bulldog," and left at some suitable spot at Cape Joseph Henry. Owing to the impossibility of depositing autumn or, indeed, any other depôts, sledge-travelling *away from a coast* has never yet been carried to any distance. We looked upon this attempt in the light of a more than doubtful experiment. It nevertheless promised a higher northern latitude than the coast-line route. When we compared notes amongst ourselves after we had started, one or two thought that N. lat. 86° might be attainable, but the majority drew the line at 85°.

On the morning of 3rd April all hands mustered for the last time on the floes beside the ship. The final preparations were complete, and our seven heavily-laden sledges lay ranged in a line, with their knotted drag-ropes stretched on the snow. When every point in their dress and outfit had been carefully inspected, the men closed together, and joined heartily in the short service read by the chaplain. All felt the serious nature of the work they were about to undertake, but nevertheless looked forward to it eagerly. Then the order was given, and the sledge crews took their places—fifty-three men and officers in all. A little group of twelve only remained by the ship, every one of them regretting that it was not their duty to share hard work and exposure with their messmates. With three cheers the men took leave of their comrades and of the gallant little ship that had so well sheltered them, and the whole

detachment moved forwards. The last to leave us was the Captain. He walked on a little while with each sledge, giving us a few words of advice or encouragement before he bade us God-speed.

For a mile or more the sledges crept slowly along in the same order as they had started, dragging through the snow with much difficulty. The whole depth of the runners buried in the soft snow made them pull, as one of the men said, "like a plough with a cart-load on it." The two leading sledges pulled the heaviest, though the weight per man was about equal in all. They carried specially-built boats, wonderfully light in proportion to their size, weighing respectively 740 and 440 lbs., but difficult to manage, because they distributed the weight over the whole length of the sledge. Every time a sledge stuck, it took a united effort with a "One, two, three, haul!" to start it forward again. Soon, in order to save the men, it became necessary to double-bank the sledges—that is to say, two crews pulled one sledge forward and then walked back for the other. Even the sledges without boats pulled very heavily. We could not but confess that the

PLATE XI.—WINTER QUARTERS, FROM AMONGST THE FLOEBERGS, LOOKING SOUTH, MARCH, 1876.—p. 50.

QUARTER of a mile north of the "Alert" a field of polar floe had been pushed on shore, and split up into a number of floebergs, with lanes and streets between them. This view of our winter quarters was obtained from the top of one of the fragments. Beyond the ship Cape Rawson may be seen forming the western portal of Robeson Channel, while away across the strait the snowy hills of Greenland make the eastern.

PLATE XII.—A FLOEBERG, SIMMON'S ISLAND, APRIL, 1876.—p. 59.

THE great stratified masses of salt ice that lie grounded along the shores of the Polar Sea are nothing more than fragments broken from the edges of the perennial floes. We called them floebergs in order to distinguish them from, and yet express their kinship to, icebergs—the latter and their parent glaciers belong to more southern regions. Partly because it was a conspicuous point to push on for before halting for lunch, the floeberg on Simmon's Island became a familiar landmark in the many trips of the supporting sledges across Black Cliff Bay; and the chill hour while tea was preparing was often spent in speculating on the enormous force required to push the huge square mass so high on shore.

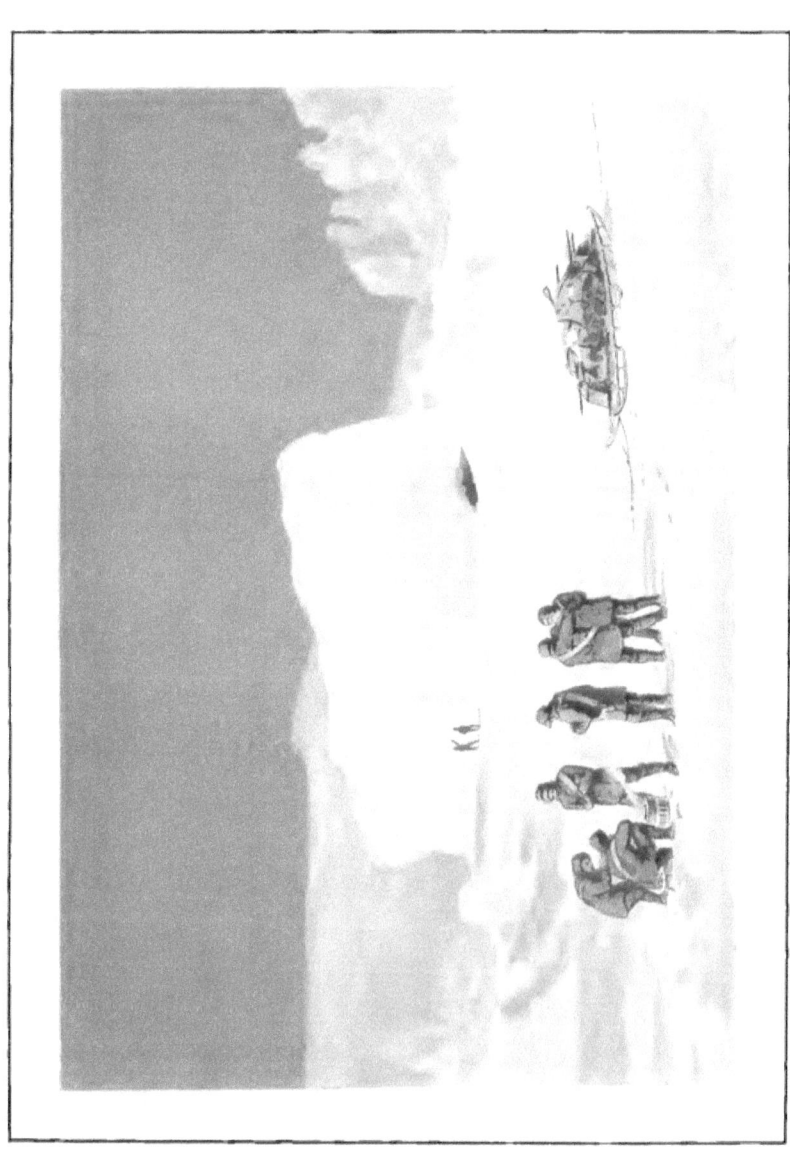

labour was harder than we had expected, but if others had gone through it we could. Crews loaded with exactly the same stores as ours, and pulling the same 240 lbs. a man, had accomplished all the longest journeys on record. Every ounce of weight on each of the seven sledges had been carefully thought over. Not so much as an unnecessary screw was carried. The sledge-rifle, for example, had four inches cut off its barrel and all the brass-work removed from its stock. Both men and officers knew that no reduction was possible unless the number of days' travel was curtailed, or some other change made in the well-tried arrangements of their successful predecessors. On one point, however, our parties deviated from precedent. Tea instead of rum for lunch was most decidedly an improvement.

We camped early on the first day's march. The spot selected was a little bay inside one of the curious hook-shaped promontories of the coast. The process of camping is a simple one. When camping-time comes, an officer goes on in advance and selects a flat piece of snow—a spot where it is soft for about six inches down is best. Then the sledge halts. Everything is unpacked. The cook of the day lights up his stearine lamp under a panful of snow for tea. The tent, with its poles already secured in it, is pitched, with its door away from the wind, and secured by ropes to the sledge at one end, and to a pickaxe driven into the snow or ice at the other; then a waterproof is spread over the snow inside, and over it a robe of duffle, a material like close blanket. The sleeping-bags and haversacks are next passed in, and the men, beginning with the innermost—for there is not room for all at once—change their snow-saturated moccasins and blanket wrappers for night pairs carried in the haversack. Moccasin, worsted stockings, and blanket wrappers all pull off together, frozen hard into one snowy mass about the foot. Meantime others are "banking up" snow all round the tent outside. Nothing adds more to the warmth of the tent than thorough "banking up." In about an hour from the time of halting, every one, except the cook, is packed inside his bag. All wear close-fitting Berlin wool helmets, enclosing head and neck, and leaving only the face exposed; the men call them "Eugénies," for they were the thoughtful gift of the Empress. The cook soon gives notice that tea is ready, and each man sits up in his bag and gets his pannikinful, softening his biscuit in it as it cools to a drinkable temperature. After tea comes half-a-pound of pemmican—a peppery mixture when one's lips are blistered with hot and cold pannikins, and cracked with sun and frost. An ounce of preserved potato is warmed up with it, and greatly improves its flavour. When the cook has trimmed his lamp for the morning, and scraped out the pannikins, his duties are over, and he changes his foot coverings, wriggles into his bag, and squeezes himself down next the door. Finally, about half a wine-glassful of rum with a little water is served out all round. This, however injurious under other circumstances, helps to tide over the chilly moments when one's frozen clothes melt, and acts much as a bellows does to a feeble fire. The heads soon disappear into the bags, and everyone goes to sleep as fast as the cold and cramp in his feet and legs will let him.

The hardships of sledging are made up of innumerable small worries. For the first two or three days we were all plagued with cramp; we could hardly bend up our knees to tie a moccasin or put on a foot wrapper without being obliged to kick out suddenly, overbalancing ourselves and our neighbours into a general mêlée, like a row at Donnybrook Fair. When the men began to get warm in their bags, muffled remarks about the cramp gradually gave place to smothered snores that would last till morning, and then the performers would wake with a firm conviction that they had never slept at all. On our first night of spring sledging the temperature fell to minus 35°, and many lay awake with the cold. Four nights afterwards it was nearly ten degrees colder, but the tents were better banked up and the under robes and coverlet better laced together; some of us, moreover, had discovered that turning the mouth of the bag under and lying on it greatly increased the warmth. The officer is the outside man at the end of the tent away from the door. It is his duty to call the cook the first thing in the morning. It is no easy thing to wake at the right hour when the sun shines impartially all the twenty-four. The watch is often consulted two or three times before five o'clock comes. Then the cook turns out, lights his lamp, has a pipe, sets some snow melting, and scrapes down cocoa for breakfast; afterwards he walks in over his sleeping companions, and brushes down the snowy festoons of frozen breath hanging from the tent.

THE DAY'S MARCH DONE.

Cocoa and pemmican are disposed of soon after seven. The frozen blanket wrappers and moccasins that have served for a pillow have to be got on again, and about eight the sledge is again ready to start. Packing is cold work, and everybody is anxious to be off and get up a little warmth with exercise.

In our next day's march we visited the snow-house built by Petersen in the autumn, and found its roof level with the snow. A fox had taken up his quarters in it, and made very free with the dog biscuit. That night we camped near a conspicuous mass of ice on the shore of a small island. The spot afterwards became a well-known landmark. Partly by accident, and partly because the striking piles of ice made a definite point to march for, the numerous shorter sledge parties often halted there for lunch or camp. Upon one such occasion the drawing reproduced in this book was obtained (Plate No. 12). The floeberg itself was not a very large one, but it afforded an excellent example of the structure of polar floe. We could not but wonder what enormous force had pushed it upwards on the sloping beach till its flat upper surface stood forty feet above the floes around it. The lower half was made of what may be called conglomerate ice, the upper was stratified with the usual white and blue layers—white where the ice was spongy with air-cells, blue in the denser layers between. High overhead might be seen a section, in olive-tinted ice, of what had once been a summer pool, and on top of all, like sugar on a cake, lay last season's snow, slowly condensing into ice.

A day's march beyond the island and its floebergs we came to a spot where many traces of game had been seen in the autumn, but after a long search, while the sledges halted to take in a depôt of pemmican, we only found one hare track, and it led down over the crest of an inaccessible cliff, so we returned to camp empty-handed. During the night we reflected that it was a pity to lose nine pounds of fresh meat without another effort; so in the morning, while the sledges were packed, we walked along the floes to a point under where the tracks had been lost, and by carefully searching the crest of the cliff with a telescope the tracks were discovered and traced downwards, along narrow ledges and abrupt slopes, to a sheltered nook, half way down the cliff, that looked utterly inaccessible to anything but a bird. There, in her sanctuary, poor pussy sat, in fancied security, till the rifle brought her tumbling downwards to the floes just as the last sledge reached the spot. This solitary hare was the only fresh food procured by our northern sledge-crews. From henceforth they were beyond the limits of game, and in this one condition our parties differed widely from those whose precedent they were attempting to follow. The longest journeys ever accomplished were made by Sir Leopold M'Clintock and Lieutenant Meecham. The former obtained forty-six head of game, including eight reindeer and seven musk oxen; the latter no less than seventy-seven head, including nine deer and four oxen.

Our party was now reduced to six sledges. The seventh returned, as had been arranged, carrying with them a man who had been an invalid since the day after leaving the ship. From this point the road lay due northward over floes half-a-mile wide, with hedges of hummocks between them. The surface looked smooth enough, but it was only a crust over soft snow, and broke under one's weight into slabs most uncomfortable to travel over. Nothing can exceed the monotony of sledge-travelling. Day after day the same routine is gone through; day after day the same endless ice is the only thing in sight. A dark stone projecting above the snow on a cape we were approaching was the only coloured thing in sight for two whole marches, and it had a most disagreeable fascination for our eyes. In order to compensate for this blankness of scenery, every man had been advised to decorate the back of his holland overall with such devices as seemed good to him. Accordingly the back view of our sledge-crews was an extraordinary spectacle. One man's back bore a large black anchor with the motto "Hold fast," another displayed a complicated hieroglyphic savouring of Freemasonry. Here was a locomotive engine careering over a beautifully green sod, and on the next back a striking likeness of the Tichborne claimant bespoke the bearer's admiration for the "distressed nobleman." Here, again, was an artistic effort which had cost its author many a week of painstaking execution, but neither he nor anyone else could tell what it was. Union-jacks, twelve-ton guns, and highly mythical polar bears, were of course common. These decorations were most useful in identifying the various men—no easy matter when all were dressed alike, and every face was swollen and blistered with sun and frost, and blackened with stearine smoke.

On 7th April, some difference of temperature in the still air treated us to a display of mirage. Almost all day long, as we marched forwards, the conical mountains of Cape Joseph Henry raised themselves up in pale shadow against the sky, and spread out into great flat table-lands, spanning the valleys with bridges, and constantly flickering into new shapes.

On the seventh day's march we crossed a floe so much raised above its fellows that it got the name of "The Castle." Its surface was about an acre in extent, and, judging from its height over the water, it could not be less than one hundred feet—perhaps one hundred and fifty—in thickness. It was walled in all round by lines of *débris*, piled upon its edges and cemented together with snow, perpendicular outside, but sloping inwards, so that the inside looked like a vast saucer. The easiest road for the sledges lay right across it. Several breaches occurred in its walls, and with the aid of picks they were soon made practicable. A sketch made as the

CREVASSE NEAR CAPE JOSEPH HENRY.

boats passed across represents a scene familiar to many of our sledge parties, for "Castle Floe" was subsequently crossed on no less than thirteen separate occasions (Plate No. 13).

Sunlight amongst the ice is often very beautiful, but at the same time very inconvenient. It had already peeled our faces, now it attacked our eyes. Every crystal of snow reflected a miniature sun, and the path of the rays seemed literally sown with gems, topaz and sapphire generally, but here and there a ruby. Similar colours, but with a curious metallic lustre like oil on water, tinted the fleecy clouds overhead, and the sun itself was almost always surrounded by circles similar to those seen round the moon in winter, but exquisitely rich and brilliant in rainbow-hued colour. No painter could hope to produce the faintest resemblance to such effects. The light was in fact altogether too bright for mortals, and we could only face it with goggles on. The gem-like gleams especially produced a quick pain in the back of the eye that considerably lessened their æsthetic effect. The officers, who have to travel well in advance and climb hummocks to find a road for

PLATE XIII.—ON THE NORTHERN MARCH, April 8, 1876.—p. 60.

ON the sixth day's march of the united northern and western parties from the ship, this sketch was outlined in pencil while the sledges passed across a floe, little if at all under one hundred and fifty feet in thickness. Like most heavy floes, its edges were piled with rubble ice, cemented and smoothed off with snow-drift, showing a perpendicular wall outside, but sloping inside to the general undulating surface. The easiest road lay right across it, and with the aid of picks a natural gap in its walls was soon converted into a practicable path. The united crews of the "Bull-dog" and "Marco Polo" are hauling the latter sledge down through the gap, while the "Challenger's" and "Poppie's" have just reached the spot with the first of their sledges.

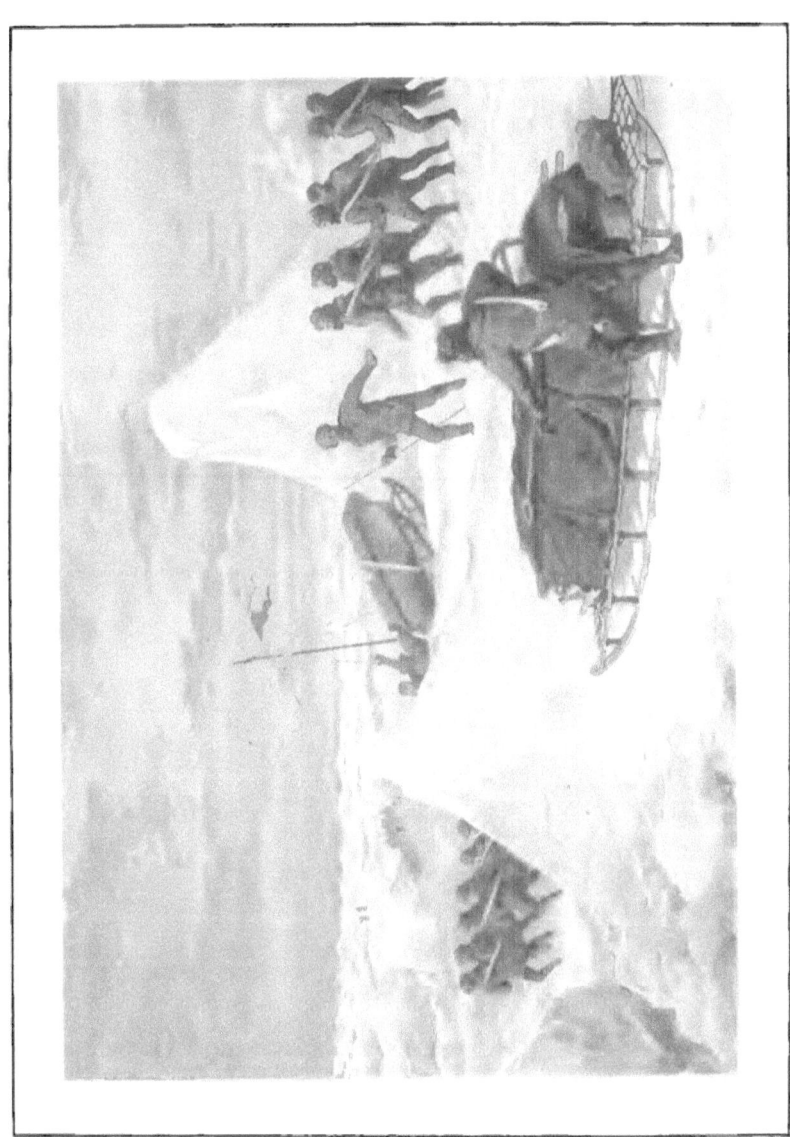

the sledges, cannot wear goggles continuously; vapour from the eye freezes on the inside of the glass, and it requires the keenest sight to detect differences of level and distance in the white blank of the prospect. On our eighth day's journey a faint mist took away all shadow from the ice, and though a man might be seen several hundred yards off, it was quite impossible to tell whether the next step was up or down, into a hole, or against a hummock. That day, pioneering was done rather by touch than sight. When the fog lifted, we found ourselves close to Cape Joseph Henry, and next forenoon the depôt left there in the autumn was transferred to the advancing sledges.

Half-a-mile northward from the depôt, a bank of snow, evidently the accumulation of ages, sloped down from a small hill to the sea. In one place a great slice of the bank had broken bodily from the mass above, leaving a deep crevasse. This was bridged over and completely concealed, except in two places, where the roof had fallen in and exposed its perpendicular walls of green ice streaked with layers of earth and sand. The bank was in fact a miniature "discharging glacier," the only one yet met with on this coast. A few yards below the openings, the bridge was strong enough to bear the heavily-laden sledges of the western parties. Their course lay through the valley to the left, for though the snow on shore was in many places soft and deep, a short cut across the isthmus promised better travelling than the crush of floes round the cape. The prospects of the northern party were less encouraging. Looking northward from the hill over the crevasse, an icy chaos spread to the horizon. Mirage every now and then raised lines and flakes of distant pack into view, but all as rough and rugged as the ice-floes at our feet.

The detachments separated on 11th April. We of the supporting sledges bade both goodbye with three cheers, and watched them slowly wind out of sight amongst the hummocks, the one to the westward, the other poleward; and as we retraced our steps on the return journey, their "One, two, three, haul!" came faintly to us across the ice.

CHAPTER IX.

News from the "Discovery"—Sickness—Peterson's Death and Burial—The Relief of the Northern Detachment—The most Northern Grave—The March to 83° N. Lat—Its Results—The Advance of the Season—Anxiety for the Safety of the Western Party—Its Return—Two Hundred Miles to the West—Further Efforts Poleward Hopeless.

MEANTIME, our friends in the "Discovery" had passed the winter in not a little anxiety about our fate. Their efforts to communicate in autumn were no more successful than ours, and as spring slipped by and no news came, the suspense increased. Could it be that the "Alert" had penetrated beyond the range of communication, or that any disaster had happened to her? It had been arranged that at the latest a party would reach the "Discovery" from her before the 1st April, and now March was nearly gone. News, however, was close at hand. The dog-sledge, "Clements Markham," had gallantly fought its way southward past the steep cliffs of Robeson Channel, and when, on 24th March, its crew rounded Cape Beechy and left the last of the cliffs behind them, they knew their troubles were over. Next day they came to a recent sledge-track, and the dogs at once struck out like hounds on a fresh scent. The last promontories were soon passed, and as Discovery Bay opened out, a cheer from the galloping sledge brought a crowd of figures racing from the ship to meet it. In a moment all were shaking hands in a storm of questions. Where was the "Alert"?—had she passed "Navy Opening" or got to "President's Land"?—and what were the prospects polewards?

The arrival of the dog-sledge was a signal for the immediate departure of the "Discovery's" sledging parties. A dog-sledge was despatched south-eastward to "Hall's Rest" to ascertain how far the stores left by U.S.S. "Polaris" could be utilised. Then two eight-men sledges, the "Sir Edward Parry" and the "Stephenson," under Lieutenant Beaumont and Dr. Coppinger, started for the north coast of Greenland, calling at Floeberg Beach on their way, and being there joined by Lieutenant Rawson's sledge, the "Discovery." They left the "Alert" on 20th April, and two smaller sledges helped them across Robeson Channel, and then left them to follow the rugged coast that we could see stretching far eastward to Cape Britannia. Another division of sledges, with Lieutenant Archer and Sub-Lieutenant Conybeare, pushed northward through Lady Franklin Sound, hoping to find it opening northward like Robeson Channel, and perhaps affording a smooth and direct route to the shores of the Polar Sea for next year's parties.

The "Discovery" had passed a winter little, if at all, less severe than ours, but in one respect she had been more fortunate. No less than thirty-three musk oxen were secured in the autumn, and thus a supply of good fresh meat was issued twice a-week during the winter. Her routine and amusements were almost identical with our own, but we heard with surprise of her

PETERSEN'S DEATH AND BURIAL.

skating rink, and of dramas performed in a snow-built theatre on shore, where a temperature many degrees below zero obliged the actors to appear muffled to several times the size of ordinary stage heroes.

After a short rest, our dog-sledge returned to the "Alert," and reached her just a day too late to give the western and northern parties news from the "Discovery." She was then at once despatched to pioneer a "high-road" to Greenland across the narrowest part of the channel in advance of the "Discovery's" detachment. From this time the arrival and departure of sledge-crews was a matter of daily occurrence.

Numerous supporting sledges, now travelling invariably in the hours called night, arrived from Greenland or Cape Joseph Henry, filled up with stores, and left again, each fully occupied with its own work, and only catching an occasional glimpse of what the others were doing.

It was while all were thus actively employed that sickness—the one sickness of the Arctic regions—appeared amongst us. No one with medical experience of the disease can read the sledge journals of former expeditions without recognising numerous indications of scurvy. Our parties, more than five hundred miles north of where Franklin was lost, and in an unexpectedly colder and more lifeless climate, had no greater safeguards than their predecessors. Accordingly, each sledge-crew that returned to the ship showed fresh examples of the exhaustion, swollen and sprained ankles, stiff knees, and bruised and painful legs, only too familiar to Arctic travellers. Petersen, already maimed by frost-bite, was its first victim. He died on 14th May, and

PETERSEN'S GRAVE.

on the 19th the few remaining on board carried him to his grave. A spot on the top of a small hill, half-way between the beach and the beacon on Cairn Hill, was chosen, because a long heavy slab, suitable for a tombstone, lay there. The ground was frozen as hard as rock, and it took three days' hard work with pick and gunpowder to dig a grave three feet deep. The slab, afterwards rough-hewn by his messmates, and an oaken tablet covered with brass, marks where he lies.

As the season advanced, signs of approaching summer began to appear. On 19th May, the temperature, for the first time in nine months, rose above freezing. Icicles formed from the projecting angles of the floebergs—and it may here be remarked that icicles, though very common in Arctic pictures, are rare in reality, for they only form in the brief interval between winter and summer, and last but a week or ten days. Signs of returning life began to multiply. A sledge party, returning from Cape Joseph Henry on 21st May, brought in two ptarmigan, snow white, but for one solitary brown feather on the hen. On 4th June, one of us found a little brown caterpillar creeping on some uncovered stones, and saw a flock of birds that looked like knots. In some places the snow was softening into discoloured patches, in others it was gradually leaving the ground. Light snow often fell, but the tiny star-shaped crystals evaporated without wetting the brown slate of the hill-tops. There was as yet no water in the ravines, but it was plain that the thaw was at hand. A sledge party that got back to the ship on 7th June experienced very unsettled weather, and had to wade through a good deal of soft slushy snow sometimes knee deep. The travelling season was fast drawing to a close, and our extended parties had evidently little time left for their return. Just before tea-time on 8th June, those of us who happened to be on board were startled by hearing Lieutenant Parr's voice in the captain's cabin. He had come alone, and we soon heard his tidings. The whole northern detachment was broken down with scurvy, and could not reach the ship without assistance, and that must be immediate. Five men were already helpless on the sledges. He had left them near Cape Joseph Henry, twenty-two hours before, and had marched in the whole way.

There was neither time nor occasion to hear more. Every soul capable of pulling at once got orders to man relief sledges. A dog-sledge, laden with immediate necessities, started in advance to cheer them with the news that help was near.

It was advisable to follow Lieutenant Parr's footprints, for, once off the track, the distressed party might easily be passed. He had called at Snow-house Point, hoping to find lamp and matches that would enable him to get a drink in the tent pitched there to assist returning parties, but a wolf had gnawed the tent ropes, and it lay flat on the snow. Near Castle Floe the tracks crossed and re-crossed in a complete maze, for there he had all but lost his way in a treacherous fog. A short halt was necessary to rest and feed the dogs, then we pushed on as before. At length, twenty-three hours after leaving the ship, we caught sight of a figure seated beside a loaded sledge, and resting his head upon his hands; then two others staggered up, helping a third between them; and a moment after, six men slowly emerged from among the hummocks dragging up a second sledge. The wind blowing from them towards us prevented them hearing our first shout, but they soon saw us, and with a faint cheer limped forward, poor fellows, to meet us. For a time our hearts were in our throats, and no one could speak much. Hardly one of them was recognisable. The thin, feeble voices, the swollen and frost-peeled faces and crippled limbs, made an awful contrast to the picked body of determined men we had seen march north only two months before. Four lay packed amongst the tent robes on the sledges—only four, for one had died soon after Parr left them. He was a private in the marine artillery, and belonged to the "Victoria" sledge. Poor Porter—George, as the men called him—had been one of the strongest and most energetic of the party. They had dragged him on the sledge thirty-nine days—others had been on longer—and his death greatly depressed both

PLATE XIV.—THE MOST NORTHERN GRAVE, JUNE, 1876.—p. 65.

A LITTLE mound of ice on the side of a floe-hill, and a rough cross made of a sledge batten and a paddle, mark our shipmate's grave—the most northern of any race or time.

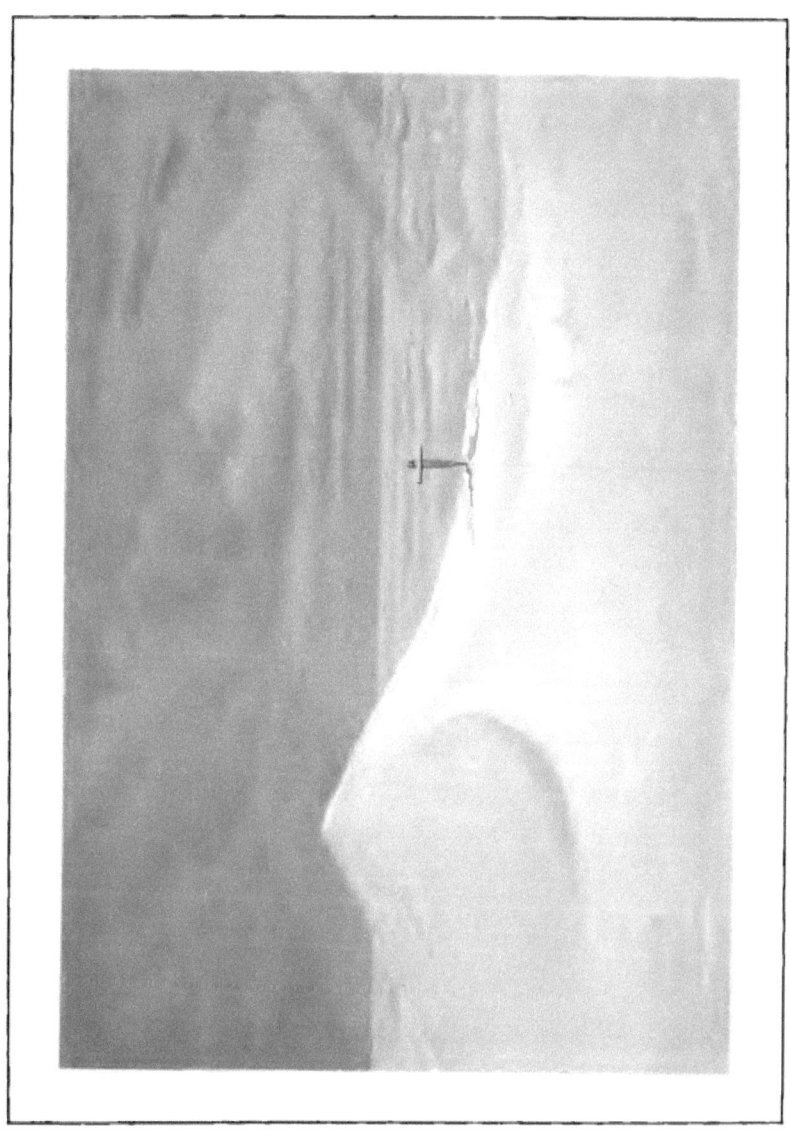

crews. They buried him deep in the ice not far from their camp, and had made one day's march southwards when we met them. The place was only a mile off, so, when the wants of the survivors had been attended to, we walked back to see it. Sunlight streaming through low clouds of drifting snow made it difficult to see far, but we soon recognised the little mound on the side of a floe-hill. A rough cross, made of a sledge-batten and a paddle, and with a text written on it in pencil, stood at the head. They could do no more for him. Perhaps the sketch reproduced in this book (Plate No. 14) may serve as a humble memento of our shipmate's grave, the most northern of any race or of any time.

The first symptoms of scurvy appeared amongst the men only a few days after the auxiliary sledges had quitted the party on the northward march; and before the expenditure of half their provisions obliged them to turn back, they had three men on the sledges, and half the detachment crippled with stiff knees. Instead of finding the floes increase in width as they left the land, they met with nothing worthy of the name of floe. Their road lay across endless hummocks of crushed fragments, piled on each other and drifted over with snow. One half the party worked in advance, slowly hewing a road with their pickaxes. The remainder toiled after them, hauling up each of the three sledges in turn. On 12th May they reached their most northern point, north latitude 83° 20′ 26″, a little less than four hundred miles from the Pole.

Considering the helpless state of the majority, we could not but think them most fortunate in being able to regain the land before even the strongest of them lost the strength and courage that carried their message to the ship. Looking at them as they staggered feebly along, panting at every breath, we forcibly realised the probable fate of those large parties from Franklin's ships that remain to this day unaccounted for. Since reaching the depôt at Cape Joseph Henry, the men had had ample supplies of lime juice, and nothing now remained but to carry them to the ship before the disruption of the pack. Immediately after falling in with them, the dog-sledge had been sent back again to carry the news of their whereabouts to the relief parties led by the Captain, and in a few hours it again reappeared, carrying a pleasant surprise for the invalids—four Brent geese, swinging by the necks from the back of the sledge. A camp, to break the journey to the ship, had been formed at a little bay in Black Cliffs, where the geese had been shot, and in a few minutes two of our invalids that could best bear the journey were packed on the sledge, and whirled off towards it behind the willing dogs. The main relief parties were soon in sight—two sledges, manned in great part by officers, Captain Nares himself pulling in the drag-ropes of the leading sledge. Thus reinforced, three marches carried the whole party back to the ship. The first instalment reached her by dog-sledge on 12th June. Next day, when Flagstaff Point was rounded, and the yards and masts of the ship were again in view, the "Marco Polo" sledge went in front. Her officer and three men had throughout steadily refused to be treated as invalids, and now, hoisting their sledge pennant and the Union Jack they had so gallantly carried to the most northern point ever reached by land or sea, they led the way alongside the ship.

Such results as were obtained by the northern party have been greatly lost sight of in the painful interest connected with the cause of the scurvy, a subject which it would be altogether improper to enter upon here. But the effort to penetrate across the polar pack has proved other facts besides the necessity for a change in sledge diet. The attempt was never a hopeful one, but if it had not been made, no one would have been satisfied that it was impossible. If the men had been able to march as far every day after the scurvy appeared as they did before it—in other words, if the scurvy had not broken out—they would have reached only twenty-seven miles further north. The Pole lay 435 miles from their most advanced depôt. Their total distance marched was 521 geographical miles, so that under impossibly favourable circumstances—if they had been able to travel in a perfectly straight line, pulling a single sledge, and with ice as smooth as a lake, they would have succeeded in reaching the Pole and half-way back again, a conclusion which would be neither satisfactory nor instructive. If a comparatively unbroken ice-cap exists, and if its surface affords better travelling than its broken margin, it is possible that some future expedition may yet find it lying nearer Cape Joseph Henry, and travel over it to 84° or 85°, but certainly not to the Pole. The broken condition of the floes is inexplicable; perhaps a small island or bank exists to the northward. Those who choose to think so have two facts to hang their faith on: a hare track was found thirty miles from the land, and the depth of the Polar Sea at the furthest camp was only seventy fathoms.

When the northern party arrived on board the ship, they found her very different to what they had left her. The thawing snow had been thrown off her upper deck, and the banking up round her sides had almost disappeared. A deep pool of not very clean water lay all round the ship, and in order to get on board it was necessary to cross a bridge some twenty feet long made of poles and planks. The tide rose and fell in this pool, showing that the ice in which the ship was imbedded was actually supported like a bridge between the shore and the floebergs; in fact, so fixed was the ship that, when the snow banking sank a little more, the tide might be seen rising and falling against the torn and ragged planking of her sides. Other pools of water lay on the floes, especially in the neighbourhood of floebergs. Cracks, too, were opening in every direction, and though there was as yet no motion in the pack, it seemed as if it only wanted a strong wind to set it grinding and roaring as it did in autumn. This state of affairs, together with the two following even more important considerations, made us very anxious about Lieutenant Aldrich and his crew. He had a good store of lime juice laid out in depôt for his return journey, but, with the experience of the northern party before us, we could hardly hope that his crew would be free from scurvy when they reached it. And again, we knew, from the reports of his auxiliary sledge, that he had penetrated far to the westward across an absolute desert of deep snow, which, if once softened, would effectually bar his return, and cut him off from assistance.

In many places round the ship the snow was softening rapidly, so much so that spots once hard enough to walk on were now totally impassable. Even snow-shoes, which had proved most useful on the march to the rescue of the northern party a week before, now balled so much under the heel, and shovelled up such a weight of slush, that they could not be used.

On clear days the depôt at Cape Joseph Henry was visible with a good glass from the top of Cairn Hill. As long as it could be seen we knew that the party had not reached it, and a most anxious watch was kept on the little flickering miraged spot. Up to the 18th June no change occurred, and then Lieutenant May and his indefatigable dogs went off to try and find some trace of the missing party. On the 25th the suspense came to an end. It was Sunday morning, and shortly after service the news came from Cairn Hill that both Aldrich's sledge and the dog-sledge were in sight. The two tents pitched on the floes near Mushroom Point could be made out plainly. They were evidently encamped for the day as usual. Their homeward march would not begin till evening, so at 7 p.m. everyone that could left the ship to meet them. Rounding a low point, we came on them suddenly. The "Challenger" led the way with colours flying and sledge-sail set. Her officer and the last man left of his crew—a stalwart, light-hearted teetotaler—hauled in her drag-belts. One man, unable to walk, lay muffled on the sledge, the others kept up as best they could, taking turns on the dog-sledge. They had turned back from a point two hundred and thirty geographical miles to the westward, and had travelled, there and back, over seven hundred miles of coast-line, but had found no shore leading poleward. On their outward journey, as they passed each successive cape, another and another came into view, till, on rounding a headland in north latitude 83°.7, they found the shore-line bending off to the southward. At this spot, since called Cape Columbia, a slaty cliff sloping downward to the floes formed the most northern point of the new world. For miles on either side the shore was lifeless, but there on the slope of the cape, amongst the stones and snow, they found a little Arctic poppy, with its tiny yellow petals withered into lines and folds of green. Beyond Cape Columbia it was sometimes hard to tell where the land ended and the frozen sea began; here and there, banks of sand and gravel were bare of snow, but when you dug into them with a pick there was deep ice beneath. On the left lay a monotonous, snow-clad shore rising into irregular mountain groups, and on the right, perennial floes, worn into mounds and valleys. They still followed the shore-line, till, on their forty-fifth day's journey, they found themselves further south than the winter quarters of the ship. Then they came to the limit of their provisions. There was only enough left to carry them back to their farthest depôt. And so, recovering in succession each of the little piles of stores deposited on their outward journey, they retraced their footsteps along this shore that no other human eyes than theirs had ever looked on. For a week before the dog-sledge met them their state was even worse than we had feared. The snow that bore them on their outward way had softened; every step sank a different depth in it, sometimes to the knee, sometimes to the waist. The men broke down one by one, strength and appetite failed them, and every motion of their swollen and stiffened limbs was an agony. They would haul the sledge five or six yards forward, and then stop for want of breath. With fifty miles of bottomless snow before them, it was no wonder some of them began to think their prospects hopeless, and wanted to be left behind rather than burden the others with their weight. But the sight of the dog-sledge put new life in the party. Its four strong men and six plucky dogs soon got them over their difficulties. Now they were safe and close to the ship, and knees grew straighter than they had been for many a day; those who could walk at all required an order to keep them on the dog-sledge. There was amongst them an ex-member of the "Bulldog" sledge, who had impressed himself specially on his former sledge-mates by one peculiar trait—he never could see a joke till hours after it was made, and then his sudden roars of laughter would sometimes wake the whole crew from their first sleep. The poor fellow was now amongst the worst, but he insisted on being helped into the drag-belts, and staggered alongside the ship in harness. Thus ended the spring sledging.

For another month hunting parties scoured the land, and two sledges tried to find an overland route to the "Discovery" in case our ship should suffer in the disruption of the pack; but so far as the "Alert" was concerned, the exploring work of the year was over. Of the "Discovery's" proceedings we yet knew little. We had heard that Lady Franklin Sound had proved a mere inlet. No news had reached us from the North Greenland detachment, but the shore that we could see from our mast-heads and from the hills of Floeberg Beach was long and deeply indented, and its extreme limit at Cape Britannia was far to the east, but little to the north.

The summer disruption of the pack was now evidently close at hand, and it was therefore necessary to come to an immediate decision about the future. We had men in both ships who had passed many winters in "whalers," and they were unanimously of opinion that the "Alert" had little if any chance of ever leaving her winter quarters. Those with knowledge of naval Arctic work thought otherwise. The "break-up," when it did come, would probably give us a choice of three alternatives—namely, to advance, to stay where we were, or to retreat. As for advancing, in some very favourable season we might perhaps get the ship about twelve miles further westward and five further north, but this was the very utmost that could be hoped for; and for all purposes of northward extension our present position was just as good. Any advance along the shores of Greenland was utterly out of the question, for the eastward motion of the pack threw its chief pressure on that shore. What, then, would another year at Floeberg Beach enable us to accomplish? Assuming, against all precedent, that our crew would completely recover and be as strong as ever they were—assuming, too, that the whole force of the Expedition, guided by the experience already gained, could be launched northwards over the floes, there could even then be no hope whatever of adding one degree to our north latitude.

Under such circumstances, retreat, if possible before the relief ship was despatched from England, became a duty. There was one objection to it that was often joked about, but of course never seriously entertained—"The public will not be satisfied unless you stay one or two more winters, or at least lose a ship." We little knew how very near we should be to doing both.

PLATE XV.—BACK FROM THE FARTHEST NORTH.—p. 65.

ON June 14th, the northern detachment, with the relief sledges sent to its assistance, returned to the ship from its ten weeks' march over the polar floes. The detachment had started northward seventeen strong, but only four remained able to pull in the drag-belts, and of these one was the officer in command. Frost-peeled and sun-burnt, with stiffened knees, and faces and clothes stained with stearine smoke, these four led the way alongside the ship, flying the Union Jack they had carried a month's hard march beyond every predecessor.

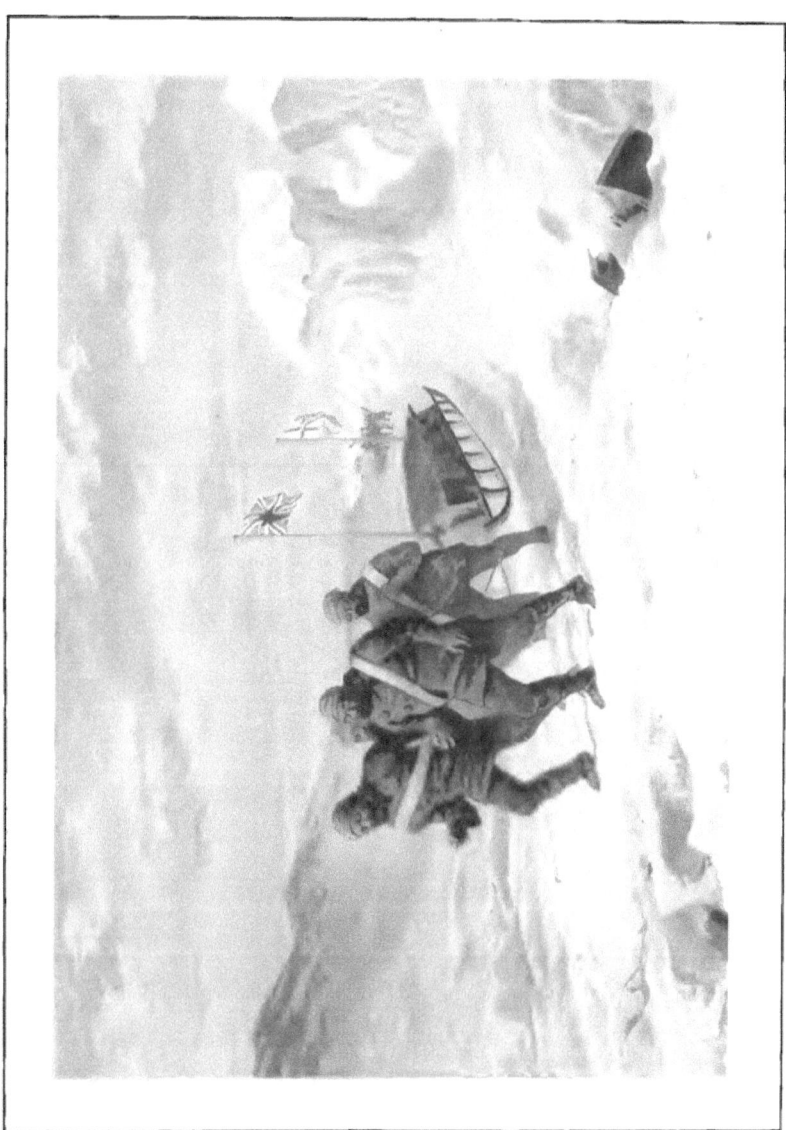

CHAPTER X.

Arctic Summer—Flowers and Butterflies—Feathered Visitors—A Strange Shot—Deceptive Game Tracks—The Land Kamsacked—No Vestige of Man—Nature's Records—The Raised Beaches—The Break-up—Farewell to Floeberg Beach—Running the Gauntlet—Robeson Channel Ice-drift—A "Nip"—Walled in by Floebergs—Escape—Re-union with the "Discovery."

UMMER at Floeberg Beach was an affair of weeks, almost of days. The turning-point came silently and quickly—not in quite the demonstrative fashion some of us expected, with an abrupt bursting forth of ravines and a general rush of torrents to the sea, but still suddenly. Three-fourths of the snow disappeared as if by magic, and the dark patches of bare land grew broader and broader every day. In some places the earth passed at once from frozen rock to dust; in others marshy spots formed, and there the whole ground was cut up into the hexagonal bosses that form a very striking feature in Arctic foregrounds. A view of Floeberg Beach from Cape Rawson (Plate No. 4), sketched on 18th July, gives an idea of how the land looked in summer. Even near the shores it is never altogether free from snow. Permanent drifts lie in the hollows, and from the crests of the cliffs at Cape Rawson a great bank several hundred feet in height sloped downward to the "mud flats" below. Trickling streams cut their way vertically down through the snow or flow in tunnels under it, then wind across the marshy flats, and end in some of the ravines that intersect the land like Lancashire "cloughs." For great part of the year the ravines are merely more or less deep grooves in the monotonous undulating whiteness, but in summer they hold brown foaming torrents rushing between steep undermined banks of snow, quite unfordable if deeper than the knee. These are the rivers of the country, but they cannot run out to sea, like ordinary streams; the grounded pack-edge prevents them; so they expend much of their energy in destroying the green one-season's ice, filling the lagoon between barrier bergs and beach. The snow was no sooner off the land than the flowers were in bloom—not very gorgeous specimens certainly, but still flowers, and with more than their share of tender sentiment, as might be seen by many bright little nosegays gathered for our invalids by the rough hands of messmates. First came close clumps of magenta-tinted saxifrage, with scarcely a trace of a leaf, and fading as fast as it bloomed; then tiny yellow *Drabas*, and white coltsfoot, and woolly willow catkins; and later, when the sorrel leaves, each as large as a sixpence, began to get red and tasteless, the yellow poppies appeared, and with them the delicately-tinted strawberry-like flowers of *Dryas octopetala*. Plants were of course few and far between—for example, four men searching all day could just gather one plateful of the valuable sorrel. All, too, were on the most Liliputian scale, seldom more than an inch above ground, but with immensely long roots. Sometimes, as we sat sketching or picking sorrel, a mosquito or two would present themselves, but they did not bite like their brethren of the Greenland settlements. A small sort of dragon-fly was not

uncommon near pools, and now and then a small brown butterfly, an *Argynnis*, or, more rarely, a yellow *Colias*, would flit by, looking somewhat incongruous amongst the rocks and snow. Birds soon became comparatively plenty; graceful grey tern fluttered about over cracks in the floes, and dipped into the pools for the little shrimps that came to the surface; flocks of knots, exceedingly wild and quick of wing, were commonly seen wading about in marshy places. A pair of snowy owls reared a brood on the cliffs of the north ravine. The parents supplied an excellent dish, and the young ones were made pets of. One of them, called "Mordecai" on account of his Asian profile, became a great favourite in consequence of his quaintly gluttonous habits. A few king-duck and Brent geese chose Grant Land as a safe nursery for their coming broods. Stringent game laws were enacted, in order that they might not be frightened away before they had made up their minds on the subject. We altogether underrated the sagacity of these creatures. Birds accustomed to winter perhaps on our own shores would of course be familiar with man, but we hoped they might take us for Eskimo armed with bows and arrows, and we were not at all prepared for their accurate knowledge of the range of Eley wire cartridge in our Guy and Moncrieff "central fires." All were not so well informed, however. One day, an officer wandering about the "mud flats" was brought to a standstill by the extreme stickiness of the ground, and was endeavouring to extract his boot from a muddy place, where it had stuck fast, when a pair of geese, impelled by most convenient curiosity, flew round him once or twice, and lit within a hundred yards, then, stretching out their necks straight in front, walked deliberately up till there was less risk of missing than of blowing them to fragments. These birds no doubt come north in search of safety for themselves and their broods during the nursing season, for the moulting of both parents, just before the young are able to fly, leaves them peculiarly defenceless. Later on, when the Expedition was on its way southward, two of our sportsmen encountered a large flock thus deprived of their pinions, and secured no less than seventy birds in fourteen shots.

A propos of shooting, the following curiously improbable personal incident is perhaps worth narrating:—One evening, shortly before the ship broke out of winter quarters, I took my rifle and went shoreward to try and find a hare, but, after a long search, was returning unsuccessful, when I happened to discover a king-duck swimming about in a small lake; there was little chance of hitting her, but she would at any rate give an excuse for a shot. After trying for twenty minutes to get within moderate range, it was plain that there was nothing for it but to walk straight up through the crunching snow; but the bird's patience was exhausted, and she rose on the wing a good hundred yards off. In sheer annoyance and chagrin I fired, when, most unexpectedly, out flew the feathers and down fell the duck. On going to pick her up, marvelling greatly at the Munchausen-like luck of the shot, and hoping that the hole was not through the best part of the bird, what was my amazement to discover that she was not only alive, but perfectly unhurt. Turn her over how I would, there was not a speck of blood on the feathers, or a scratch on any part of the body. At last the secret was discovered; the bullet had clipped the pinions off one wing, and the fall had stunned the bird. She afterwards lived some time in captivity in a hen-coop, and laid two eggs.

We had not spent many days roaming over our newly uncovered lands, before we began to suspect that tracks of game were, in our part of the Arctic regions at any rate, extremely misleading. On the way northward, whenever the ship came to a standstill amongst the floes, men and officers often made hurried visits to the shore, and invariably came off with the stereotyped report that "traces of game were numerous and recent." We found so many traces and so little game that the phrase acquired an inverted meaning, and passed into a proverb, but the discrepancy remained unaccounted for. At Floeberg Beach tracks of game were certainly numerous enough. The hard frozen mud at the margins of every pool showed footprints of birds, often so sharp and distinct that "rubbings" with pencil and paper were easily made of them, and sometimes in relief where dust had filled the impression and ice evaporation afterwards lowered the mould. In some places tracks of musk oxen were abundant, and of every size, from the little round footprints of calves to the broad hoof-marks of full-grown animals; but there was absolutely no way of telling when or in what numbers the game had been there. Once frozen, a footprint may last indefinitely, especially if protected by snow; and, for aught we could prove to the contrary, some of the tracks may have been as old as the celebrated mammoth frozen up in the Siberian mud. On 5th July, however, those who contended that the tracks were practically fossil were confounded by the appearance of three musk oxen on a hill-top beyond the north ravine. Their discoverer instantly sent off news to the ship, and, very judiciously, waited patiently till the arrival of assistance rendered their escape impossible. A few mornings afterwards, a fine bull walked innocently down to the beach near the ship, and was forthwith slaughtered. Being a good specimen, and close at hand, he was transferred to the naturalist, and he now represents his species in the British Museum.

All through the earlier weeks of July the pack gave warnings of approaching disruption. Decided motion first occurred on 16th, and on 21st the old familiar sound of "breaking plates" came from the offing, and with a loud crack the ship suddenly righted herself from the heel towards shore, which had slowly increased during the winter. Nevertheless, as long as it remained calm no important movement was likely to occur, except at high tide. We were, therefore, still able to extend our hunting expeditions to several days from the ship. It was not the search for game only, exciting as it was, that made these late trips interesting. Our hunters enjoyed a privilege that has rarely fallen to the lot of any discoverers in either past or recent times—they traversed a shore never before trodden by the foot of man. Everywhere south of the steep cliffs of Robeson Channel some vestiges of humanity were discoverable; a broken sledge-runner, a chipped flint, or a musk ox bone broken to extract the marrow, told us that wandering Eskimo had been before us; but from the cliffs northward all traces ceased—no savage hunter had ever disturbed the ice-borne boulders of Floeberg Beach to fasten down his tent of skins, or form a rough hearth for his travelling camp, and no sledges but our own were ever launched towards the icy horizon beyond—

"We were the first that ever burst
Into that silent sea."

Yet though there was no trace of man or his doings, Nature had left deeply significant records of her own to tell the history of the land. The neighbourhood of the ship was rich in such evidences. No one could walk over the broad "mud flats" half-a-mile inland from the ship without being convinced that the land had risen from the sea at, geologically speaking, no very distant period. Shells similar to those still living in the sea two hundred feet below lay strewn in abundance on the fine sand. Here a pair of valves, enormously thickened to bear the crush of ice, there a whole bed of slighter shells, still covered with their brown filmy skins, and connected by their gristly hinges. The mud itself was so salty, that where it dried in the sun a white briny coat formed on its surface. Stems and roots of laver sea-weeds were sometimes picked up, but the most interesting and eloquent witnesses of the past were the splinters and logs of driftwood that lay imbedded in the mud, or scattered along the crests of these raised beaches. The wood was easily recognised by the microscope as the wood of pine trees, and though probably very many centuries old, was often so apparently fresh as to smell woody when cut. It was not for us to conjecture when or where that wood had grown, or how it had drifted to its present elevated site; but we could not help thinking that it told of a time when the shores, though perhaps far more deeply laden with glaciers, were washed by a less ice-bound sea.

At one o'clock in the morning of 23rd July, the pack broke from the shore under the influence of a strong wind, and left pools of water outside our barrier bergs, but the ice still crushed close on Cape Rawson, and when the wind lessened, all closed in. Again, on the evening of 26th a space of water formed outside the bergs, and in order to be ready when an opportunity for a rush southward should offer, we set about breaking a channel through the floes between the ship and the nearest gap in the wall of grounded bergs. The ice was far too thick for even our longest and heaviest ice-saws, but with the aid of three hundred pounds of gunpowder, judiciously disposed in torpedoes made of tin cans and lime-juice jars, it was shattered, piece by piece, and as each mass broke off and floated free, it was pushed out to seaward by the united efforts of the whole crew wielding levers and ice-poles.

While we lay waiting for a path southward to open, we could not but look forward to the ordeal before us with a good deal of anxiety. Once round Cape Rawson, there would be no turning back. Thirty miles of shelterless cliff must be passed before we reached Lincoln Bay, and for the whole of that distance the ship would have to run the gauntlet through a mere fissure between a perpendicular wall of ice-foot, and a moving, irresistible mass of floe eighty feet and more in thickness. If fortune did not favour us, the destruction of the ship was certain, and every preparation was made to meet such an eventuality. Provisions and sledges were piled on deck ready to launch on the floes, and notes and sketches and carefully-selected specimens were packed into the smallest possible bundles, so that they could be pushed hastily into a pocket if it should be necessary to desert the ship. Early on the morning of 31st, an unusual sound awoke us; a strong breeze whistled and sung in the rigging overhead, and a low vibration, like the bass notes of an organ, filled the ship. It came from our heating boilers—steam was being got up. On deck one glance round told us that the time had come. A long black canal of water skirted the coast as far as we could see towards Cape Rawson, and the rush through it must be made now or never. Screw and rudder were already down in their places, and the sails "bent," ready to be loosed. A few strong charges of gunpowder shook the ship from her icy bed. The order "full speed ahead" was given. The screw flung a stream of foaming water over the ice, and the ship moved slowly forward into the channel blasted for her. Then, as she swung round under steam and sail through the narrow portal in the wall of bergs, we caught our last glimpse of Floeberg Beach. Shadows of clouds chased each other down over the brown slopes. The headstone of Petersen's grave stood out like a solitary human figure, and a piece of canvas fluttered on a pole over "the doctor's garden," where mustard and cress were just beginning to appear above ground. Our tall cairn on top of the hill remained in sight for a few minutes longer, then the bend of the coast shut it from view. At full speed we flew past the well-known headlands so often painfully rounded with tired crew and heavy sledge, past the ice-rounded rocks of Cape Rawson, the tower-like buttresses of Half-way Cliffs, and the dark precipices of Black Cape; but before we got to Cape Union our career was cut short—the angle of a floe lay right across our narrow path, and we had to wait in anxious inactivity till the next tide moved it off and let us slip past. All that night and next morning, the floes, closing in behind us, literally hunted us along the coast from one little hollow of the ice-foot to another. Over and over again the ship had to be pushed and wriggled through desperately narrow gaps to avoid the closing floes behind her. Several times there was so little space to pass that our boats, hoisted high up at the davits, scraped along the perpendicular wall of ice-foot. The accompanying etching is

RUNNING THE GAUNTLET.

from a sketch made near midnight on 2nd August, looking back along our track, but no sketch can convey an idea of the chief feature of the scene—the majestic and irresistible motion of the ice-fields.

Two days later, when we lay walled in by bergs in "Shift Rudder Bay," we could look back past Cape Beechey into the strait from which we had escaped, and watch the tight pack of ice islands streaming south from Robeson Channel into Hall's Sea, without the distracting influence of immediate danger, and we one and all came to the conclusion that, as an impressive example of magnificent and imposing force, no other natural phenomena could equal it. Our little vessel went very near leaving her bones on the shores of this same bay. When we reached it, the ice was closing in. A line of grounded bergs lay along the beach, with a gap in it just large enough to admit the ship. Into this we thrust her, feeling thankful for so good and opportune a shelter, but unfortunately the gateway of our castle had no portcullis to close behind us, the ice followed us in, and, foot by foot, forced the ship up on the ice-foot, heeling her over and damaging her rudder. At four in the morning the pressure suddenly relaxed, and the ship fell two feet, but remained imprisoned. For days not a patch of water was to be seen, though the whole pack moved south with one tide and halted with the next. On 8th August it blew a gale, and the ice swept past with increased speed. One large, dome-shaped fragment of polar floe crushed through our gateway, and though it grounded long before getting near the ship, the pressure behind was so enormous that it continued to advance, shovelling round lumps of ice as big as a house on either side of it, and rising out of the water as it did so, till it came against the side of the ship. Now we were nipped in earnest. First a rattle on deck, exactly like a hail-storm overhead, as the pitch cracked and flew out of the seams; then a crunch as the ship yielded, then an interval, and then another horrible vibrating crunch—for downright unpleasantness, not even the tear of a shot through a ship's timbers can compare with such a sound—but the decks did not buckle up under our feet, and the sides did not collapse. The "Alert" was evidently not fated to be destroyed in that way. Nevertheless, when the crush ceased, her position was far from comfortable; she was raised four feet by the stern and completely imprisoned in a citadel of bergs, apparently as hopelessly walled in as she well could be. There might be oceans of water outside, but how was she to get out? One chance only remained. It might be possible to make our jailor berg float by digging off the whole top of it; so all hands set to work, and for three days all that gunpowder, pick, and shovel could do was done. Time was everything, for the tide fell lower every day. At last our enemy gave up the fight, floated up, turned partly over, and sailed out through the gate, considerably smaller than when he came in. Victory came just in time; the ice opened before us across the bay and down the coast. Ice navigation is never very rapid work, every mile has to be fought for. We were only twenty-five miles from the "Discovery," but it took two days of sleepless activity to accomplish that distance, and it was late on the evening of the 11th when we rounded Distant Cape and caught sight of our sister ship.

ESKIMO BIRD-SHELTER.

CHAPTER XI.

Serious News—The North Greenland Detachments—The Missing Sledge-crews—Drifting with the Polar Pack—A Forced March of Thirty-two Hours—"Chatel's Grotto" and the "Coal Mine"—Climate Past and Present—The Return Southward—A Pool in Kennedy Channel—Race against Winter—New Ice—Out Fires—The North Water at Last—The "Pandora's" Depôt—News from Home—Conclusion.

THERE were no joyful demonstrations when the "Alert" steamed across Discovery Harbour and anchored beside her consort. Congratulations were misplaced in the face of the news which had reached us while we yet lay imprisoned at Shift Rudder Bay—news so serious that we could think or speak of little else. The last of the "Discovery's" sledge parties had not returned.

Leaving their ship on the 6th of April, 1876, and re-provisioning their sledges from the "Alert" on the 20th, her parties had crossed over Robeson Channel to the south-eastward, and reached the Greenland coast at a point twelve miles north of the spot where Hall's cairn and record marked the most northern position attained by the sledges of the American Expedition. The "Discovery's" crews may therefore be said to have begun their sledging where their gallant predecessors left off. The shore led to the north-east, and was piled with ice. Their path lay along banks of drifted snow, so steep that it was necessary to dig a groove for the landward runner of the sledge, to prevent it slipping down into the trenches and moats cut by the wind round the piles of sea-ice. These trenches were sometimes forty feet deep. When they were thirty-four days out from their ship, they arrived at the end of the continuous land, and here their last supporting sledge turned back, and left Lieutenant Beaumont's sledge, the "Sir Edward Parry," to proceed alone. Islands with steep cliffs lay before them, separated by broad fiords. Looked at from the cliffs above them, the fiords promised good travelling, for inside the line of heavy polar floes their surface was one level sheet of snow. But, unfortunately, the treacherous snow was soft. Sledge and men sank deep at every step. Pulling out each foot was like pulling off a boot, and sometimes the men preferred to creep on hands and knees rather than attempt to walk. Their ankles swelled and knees became stiff. Not a vestige of game of any sort cheered their journey. On their forty-fifth day out they had crossed the third and broadest of the fiords, and their waning stock of provisions warned them to return. For many days fog and constant snow closed in their prospect, but from a mountain nearly four thousand feet high they got a view of Cape Britannia and the islands about it far to the north-east, nearly in north latitude 83°.

The disorder which had weakened us, did not spare them. On their outward journey James Hand had been taken ill, and sent back with the supporting sledge. Poor fellow! he only lived to reach Polaris Bay. On the twelfth day of the homeward march a seaman named Paul fell helpless in the snow, and had to be carried on the sledge. Four days afterwards another took the place beside him. Soon every day added to the number of the sick, and when the party was yet forty miles from the depôt at Polaris Bay, but two, one of whom was the officer, were left to pull the others on, one by one. The advance of the season increased the misery of their position. Thawing snow fell constantly and soaked their clothes, a storm blew down their tent, and they could only spread the canvas over their sick sledge-mates and crouch under the edge, wet through and sleepless, for days at a time. At this stage, most opportune and unexpected relief reached them.

The auxiliary and Petermann Fiord parties camped at Polaris Bay fortunately divined their condition, and two officers, with Hans the Eskimo, took a dog-sledge northward to meet them. With this aid the invalids were soon carried into camp, but help came too late for one of them; a few hours after reaching camp, Charles Paul was laid beside his messmate, not far from the grave of Captain Hall of the "Polaris." The tents were pitched near a small wooden hut left by the Americans. Its roof had been disturbed by the wind, but the stores of ham, molasses, lime-juice, biscuit, and pemmican packed inside were serviceable, in spite of the five years they had lain there. A mattress found there made a luxurious bed for one of the invalids, and the members of the little colony made themselves as comfortable as circumstances would permit, while they waited for the sick to recover sufficiently to travel across to their ship, Hans meantime keeping them well supplied with seal meat. The dog-sledge carried news of their state across, and the assistance which arrived soon afterwards enabled a first detachment to leave on 29th July and reach the "Discovery" without difficulty.

The party remaining behind consisted of Lieutenant Beaumont, Dr. Coppinger, and seven men. The invalids amongst them were rapidly gaining strength; another week, if the floes would only last so long, would leave them strong enough to attempt the march, and it was arranged that they would push across the pack on the 4th of August at the latest.

This was the last that was known of the party.

It was nine in the evening of the 11th when the "Alert" steamed into Discovery Harbour, and up to that date nothing had been seen of the missing men. The recent storms and the break-up of the ice had made an awful change in their prospects. The floes, scored with the sledge-tracks of twenty-one journeys, had moved off to the south, and a tumbling, heaving mass of polar pack now filled the strait from shore to shore.

Look-out parties had already been despatched to the mountain-tops overlooking the strait, and we anxiously watched for the flag that would announce the discovery of the sledge-crews. With a vivid recollection of the Robeson Channel drift before us, we could not calmly contemplate the possibility that they had already started and been swept off south in the breaking-up pack. In such a case sudden destruction would be a merciful fate. There was still hope that they had not yet left the shore, and that if one of the ships could be forced across they might be rescued. Accordingly the "Alert" was got ready. Such of her men as were not yet strong enough for the roughest work were transferred to the "Discovery," none but working hands were kept on board, and all our little valuables—journals, specimens, and so forth—were handed over to safe keeping.

On the night of the 12th and morning of the 13th the attempt was made, but the full steam power of the ship was utterly helpless against the ponderous ice. It was simply impossible to bore even one half-mile into a pack of such proportions, and we were obliged to turn back and wait for a chance opening. Some hours before we made this attempt, a messenger had come down the hill with a report that the two tents had been made out with the telescope still pitched on the shore of Thank God Harbour, Polaris Bay. The signalman even thought he could distinguish figures passing to and fro between them, but the wish was father to the thought: we afterwards learnt that neither tents nor men were there; the party had really left that shore five days earlier, and embarked on the most extraordinary journey of this, or indeed of any other expedition.

They had made every preparation to leave on Friday, 4th August, but when that day came, the weather suddenly changed, and storms of snow and wind made travelling impossible. It blew hard all that night, and Saturday morning brought no change; everything beyond a few yards from the tents was hidden in drifting mists of fog and snow. Thus for four days they lay weatherbound. At length, on the morning of the 8th, the sun shone through the clouds, and the wind lessened, till towards evening it fell quite calm. But as the fog and mist cleared away and let them see farther and farther across the channel, they saw that all was changed. Miles of water spread between them and the white line of pack that lay under the edge of the fog.

This was well, for water is easier to travel over than ice. Their boat was soon launched and packed with necessary stores, and by tying empty spirit tins to the sledge they converted it into a raft and towed it behind. They had to be very careful, for the gunwale of their heavily-laden boat was only three inches out of water. Fortune favoured them, several good leads of open water were found amongst the floes, and by half-past two o'clock next afternoon they had pulled their boat and sledge through water-spaces and over floes to within ten miles of the opposite shore, then, tired with the long journey, and well satisfied with the progress made, they camped on a broad piece of old floe. The men were soon in their bags and asleep, but their leader had noticed a slight change in the appearance of the coast, and an unpleasant suspicion kept him wakeful. Once and again he crept out of the tent to have another look at the familiar bays and headlands. There was soon no doubt about it, the outline *was* changed, and they were further off. While they slept, the floe was fast carrying them back the way they had come. They must instantly start again, and by hard marching make up for the loss. They were soon under way, and all night toiled on over one floe after another, through pools and lanes of water, across spaces of broken rubble, and pasty bottomless sloughs of neither ice nor water. For fourteen hours they held out, then the men could do no more, rest and food were absolute necessities, but, on camping, they found to their dismay that the drift had been faster than their march, and they were four miles further off than when they started. Eleven hours slipped by in sorely needed but sorely begrudged rest, and when they next started the full danger of their situation was plain to all. They could no longer see into Lady Franklin Sound. The headlands of Cape Lieber had already hidden Miller Island, and were fast closing past Discovery Bay and Bellot Island. They were gliding helplessly into Kennedy Channel, and their provisions were already far spent. On holding a short consultation, it was resolved to relinquish any attempt to outmarch the drift of the pack, and that the only chance of safety lay in making a push across the drift for the nearest point of land, and never stopping till they reached it.

It was eight in the evening when they once more moved forward on this final effort, and for nine hours they made fair progress, but then a change came, a strong wind sprang up against them and hurried the pack still faster away from shore. Presently the floes, forced by both wind and tide, began to move with alarming violence, wheeling and turning in a most perplexing way, so that the men over and over again crossed their own track. They were now sixteen hours on the march, and every hour the land looked more distant, but they still fought on, with every thought concentrated on hurrying on at full speed. If they had stopped to consider it, there was not at this time the faintest human possibility of reaching the land against the ice-drift. But their misfortunes had reached a climax; at one in the afternoon of the 11th the wind veered to the opposite direction, and came on to blow hard. The wheeling and tossing of the floes greatly increased, but the fatal drift was checked. Providence had given them this chance, and they one and all determined to make the most of it, so, redoubling every effort, they pushed on for the land. Some fell asleep as they pulled in the drag-belts, and when they reached the edge of the pack and launched their boat, others slept at the oars. But finally, at seven in the morning of the 12th of August, land was reached, and they flung themselves down on the beach at Cape Lieber after an unprecedented march of thirty-two consecutive hours. When they had rested at this point, they had but to cross Lady Franklin Strait to reach the ships. The distance was about twelve miles, and the floes comparatively stationary. One march brought them more than half-way over, and just as they began the second, shouts and cheers coming to them across the ice heralded the arrival of a strong party from the "Alert." They had been seen by our look-outs, and were all soon on board, and never were guests more welcome. Next day, 15th August, they reached their own ship, after an absence of no less than 130 days.

Both ships were now free to voyage southward as soon as the ice would let them leave Discovery Harbour. Bellot Island formed a sort of natural breakwater, and kept the floes outside, so that the bay all round the ships was often almost clear of ice, but beyond the island the pack showed little disposition to let us through. In Lady Franklin Strait, promising-looking lines of water wound amongst the floes in many directions, but they were only ⌒⌒ shaped cracks thawed wide at the surface, and mere fissures six or eight feet under water. Looked down on from the cliffs of the island, they marbled the white floes with veins of green, very different from the inky blackness of real leads. But that the rapid approach of winter made escape less likely every day, we were well content to wait our opportunity, for there were many places in the neighbourhood of the "Discovery's" winter quarters that we of the "Alert" were anxious to see. First amongst these was the coal seam discovered by her naturalist, Mr. Hart. This was only about four miles off amongst the hills to the north, but, unfortunately, in such an inaccessible position that little more than a few pounds weight of the fuel could be brought down to the ship. Coal so far north was such a curiosity, and the fossils found near it told such a strange story, that everyone wanted specimens, and there was no difficulty in getting up a strong party to visit the "mine." So one morning a large boat-load of eager geologists, armed with picks and hammers, crossed the mouth of the harbour. Like the "breakwater" of Bellot Island, the spot where we landed bore traces of a visit from Eskimo at some very far-off time. A collection of stones marked by fire, splinters of burnt drift-wood and fragments of bones broken to get the marrow out, told plainly of some wandering hunter's camp-fire. Half-a-mile further on, one of our party picked up a fragment of a human thigh-bone, brown and weather-worn and gnawed by foxes. Strange to say, we could not find any other part of the skeleton.

Striking inland, we passed through a number of valleys with steep rocky walls and a flat floor between, like railway-cuttings on a large scale, and at length reached a little stream winding eastward towards the channel. Following it down a short distance, we found it entering a gorge, with mountains a thousand feet high on either side. Soon the only way to advance was by

AN ARCTIC COAL-SEAM.

wading amongst the boulders in the bed of the stream, with overhanging walls of black rock on either side, so close that we could almost touch both with outspread hands. No wonder the "Discovery's" autumn sledge-crews had found this a rough road. Finally, the ravine ended in a very unexpected manner. A vast bank of snow and ice sloped across from mountain to mountain, and the stream disappeared under it and into an icy cave. We followed the stream, and found ourselves in Chatel's Grotto, so called after a blue-jacket in the autumn sledge-party that had pronounced it a most comfortable camping-place. The roof was of white ice, streaked with veins of sand, and groined into all sorts of fantastic shapes. An opening overhead let in some rays of light through festoons of icicles as thick as a man's body. On either side curious sloping shelves of ice projected out over the stream. It was decidedly a picturesque spot, and if the water in which we stood had not been so intensely cold, we might have taken longer time over our sketch. Here we were close to the coal-seam, but the worst part of the road was yet

CHATEL'S GROTTO.

to come. The stream passed out of the far end of the grotto through a dark tunnel, so low that we had to stoop to avoid knocking our heads against the ice of the roof, and so dark that we were obliged to feel our way along by the sides, stumbling and floundering amongst the pools and boulders. Presently, however, light shone through at the other end, and we emerged into a continuation of the gorge. A bend of the stream brought us to the spot we sought. Right and left rose two great mountain slopes, with the rivulet running between them. The lower twenty or thirty feet of the right bank was a perpendicular wall of coal, streaked with yellow sulphurous lines. The surface had become brittle by exposure to the weather, but a few blows of a pick revealed a depth of shining black fuel, to all appearance as good as any we had on board.

Everyone was differently impressed by the great store of mineral wealth that lay before us. "What a pity we cannot get up a company and issue shares!" said one. "How comfortably we might winter alongside of this!" thought another; and a third, making a free use of the scientific imagination, pictured to himself the conditions which must have existed when this coal was waving forest, and wondered how the trees managed to live through the long darkness of winter. That they did live and flourish on this spot there was abundant proof. Mere driftwood has before now been mistaken for evidence of Arctic vegetation, but here there could be no such error. It was only necessary to cross the stream a little lower down, and split open the soft, dark slates of the opposite cliff, to find the leaves of ancient forests as perfect as when they fluttered down from the stems that bore them. The commonest were those of a cone-bearing tree allied to the great Wellingtonias of Western America, but leaves like aspen and poplar were not unfrequent. How different the climate must have been when these trees grew! Now, there is no forest within a thousand miles, and in the whole land the nearest approach to a tree is the dwarf willow, not three inches high, sheltering its tiny stem in the crevices amongst the stones.

Though the discovery of this coal-bed was most important in a scientific point of view, it was of no practical use to us. If any other expedition ever passes through Smith's Sound, we may be sure it will not be forgotten. There it remains, an inexhaustible reservoir of force, ready for anyone who can invent a new method of travelling to the Pole.

While our two ships lay waiting for a chance of escape from Discovery Bay, we began to be impressed with the fact that it was one thing to decide on the return of an expedition from a point so far north, and quite another to accomplish it without a second winter. Even yet the ships were farther north than any of their predecessors had wintered. Where many a good ship had failed, ours might not succeed. We were yet one hundred and ninety miles north of where Kane was at last compelled to abandon his ship. The "Polaris," a steamer at least as well fitted for ice-work as either of our ships, left her ribs and timbers more than two hundred miles to the south. British expeditions entangled in the ice of the Parry Group had more that latitude to contend with, but the "Resolute" was abandoned 280, the "Investigator" 450, and the "Erebus" and "Terror" 700 miles to the south of our position. The strong set through Smith's Sound was greatly in our favour, but nevertheless two hundred miles of ice-choked channel lay between us and the head of Baffin's Sea, and beyond it Melville Bay would still separate us from the most northern Danish settlement. Young ice was already forming where the floes were still, and a little more delay would compel us to pass an objectless, inactive winter where we were, and trust to next year for a better chance of return. No one in either of our ships had at this time a doubt of our success, but nevertheless such considerations had their weight. There was accordingly a general feeling of relief on board when, on the evening of 18th August, the officer of the watch reported that Captain Nares, who had as usual climbed to the top of the island, was holding out both his arms as a signal to get up steam in both boilers. The gate of pack to the southward showed some signs of opening, and we might get through by pushing amongst the broken ice between the floes. But the inertia of the fragments was too much for the ships even charging at full speed, and we were forced back to the shelter of the island with the second rudder badly damaged.

PLATE XVI.—THE LAST OF THE PALEOCRYSTIC FLOE, KANE'S OPEN POLAR SEA, CAPE CONSTITUTION, FRANKLIN AND CROZIER ISLANDS IN THE DISTANCE, AUGUST 20, 1876.—p. 81.

AS the ships returned southward, they steamed through a large "polynia," or water-space, in Kennedy Channel. It was on a still night, late in August, and the ice-locked sea was calm enough to be the veritable "Peace Pool." A few last fragments of polar floe lay here and there in the water, strangely reflected, and a dovekie swam beside one of them. Far away to the east, between Franklin and Crozier Islands, Cape Constitution rose above a faint line of pack. It was Kane's farthest point. From its base, Morton, looking on another such polynia, had naturally enough reported an open Polar Sea. The sea was open now as far southward as could be seen from the crow's nest, and yet both ships were in difficulties before morning, and a hundred miles of Smith's Sound pack still separated them from the North Water and from home.

Better fortune awaited the next effort, and on the morning of the 20th the ships fought slowly across Lady Franklin Strait. Cape Baird and Cape Leiber were passed in comparatively open water, then the ice became less and less, and as midnight approached we were astonished to find ourselves nearly sixty miles on the homeward journey, and still steaming full speed. The scene we passed through just at this time was one not easily forgotten. Under the cold yellow light of northern afterglow, Kennedy Channel lay open as far as we could see, a sheet of mirror-like water in that absolute calm peculiar to ice-locked seas. There was some low mist at the other side of the channel, probably floating over pack; through it we could distinguish the islands named after Franklin and Crozier, and between them rose Cape Constitution, the bold headland from which Morton had looked upon Kane's open Polar Sea (Plate No. 16). As we stood on deck attempting to preserve some record of the tender tints of sea and sky in water-colour, a last fragment of heavy pack floated by, and the only dovekie we had seen for many a day swam beside it.

"Open water as far as the eye can reach" really means nothing more than that there are no ice-fields within three or four miles, and yet on that limited fact alone voyagers have more than once reported that they might have sailed to the Pole or near it. The open sea off Cape Constitution was a mere pool. Before morning both ships were arrested in dense pack, and forced to retreat for shelter to a narrow inlet with steep shelving sides. We were just moored to some pieces of grounded ice, and were congratulating ourselves on the security of our refuge, when a fragment of drifting floe caught against the "Alert" and pushed her on shore under a steep ice-foot at the very top of high tide. As the water fell, her bows were left high and dry on the beach, so that a man might have crept under the front of her keel, and she fell over so much on her side that a total capsize down the sloping beach seemed not impossible; but when the tide rose again she righted, and the whole crew, straining vigorously on the capstan, dragged her off from her perilous position.

From this point southward to the entrance of Smith's Sound the return of the Expedition was one monotonous struggle with the ice. Day after day the ships pushed onward between the floes and the shore in whatever openings the changing tide made for them, sheltering behind every projection of the coast. In the far north there are very few, if any, true icebergs, but opposite the Humboldt Glacier we again encountered them, and often found a refuge from the pack amongst groups grounded near shore.

Our progress southward was a race against rapidly approaching winter. Snow fell in large quantities, and lay in thick paste on the water in cracks and pools. One by one the headlands passed on our northward voyage were rounded, and day by day new ice grew thicker and our stock of fuel dwindled. Three several attempts were made to force a way past Cape Hawkes, and when we did succeed, the bay beyond was found full of new ice, so thick that the whole power of our engines could not push through. It cracked here and there before the ships, but soon brought both to a standstill, and the order was given to put out the fires.

The bay in which we thus found ourselves arrested was afterwards called after Professor Allman. It is an indent in the western coast-line of Kane's Sea, immediately north of Hayes Sound. It is five miles wide, and at its head we could see a large glacier pouring in two streams round a snow-covered hill, and fronting the bay in a line of icy cliff. Snow lay deep on the mountains on either side, and it still snowed constantly; decks and rigging were covered; a more wintry prospect could hardly be conceived. It was already beginning to grow dark in the evenings, and lamps and candles were again in use between decks. But for a certain disappointment in being checked when we had made up our minds to return, few on board our ships were unwilling to face another winter. Here, two hundred miles further south, it would be a very different affair from the last. Release from the ice next season could be looked forward to as a certainty, and even with a stock of coal lessened by the exigencies of a second winter it would still be possible to escape from Smith's Sound. If the ships could be got into shelter near the deserted Eskimo hunting-grounds of Norman Lockyer Island, we should probably get plenty of game. Almost all our invalids were again in good health, and when spring came the smooth floes would make the exploration of Hayes' Sound a pleasure trip. Moreover, if a second winter was unavoidable, there was another reason—a somewhat ignoble one perhaps— why it would not be unwelcome. The advance of pay liberally granted by the Admiralty before sailing was not yet defrayed, and if we reached England this year almost all the men would still be in debt to the Crown, and sailors naturally prefer to land with a little money in their pockets.

We were not fated, however, to spend another season in the ice. Some motion in the floes occurred on 6th September, and the opportunity was not let slip. The remains of the coal were once more drawn upon to light the engine fires, and the ships were soon pushing through the thin floe towards some water-spaces near Norman Lockyer Island. The "Discovery" led

ALLMAN BAY.

the way, for the shape of her bow enabled her to glide up on the ice till her weight broke down through it, and she thus advanced with a sort of pitching movement.

Next day the whole south was dark with storm clouds. If the wind came, it would soon clear the channel. It did come, but only as a gentle breeze; its work was done before it reached us, and the gateway of Smith's Sound lay open. The swell coming from the south told of a long stretch of open water. Our leader might at last come down from his post in the "crow's nest;" his almost sleepless vigil was over, for his two ships were once more safe in the "North Water."

As it grew dark on the night of the 9th September, Cape Isabella, at the western side of the entrance of Smith's Sound, came into view. We knew that this was one of the points where letters might perhaps have been deposited for us, and the ships were hove-to under the wild, steep rocks, while a boat was called away to search the depôt. It soon left the ship, and disappeared in the dusk. Fearing disappointment, we tried to persuade ourselves that there was really very little chance of letters being left at this particular spot. After a while the boat reappeared. We could scarcely dare to hope, but in a few minutes bundles of letters and newspapers were being eagerly distributed. The gallant little "Pandora" had been working hard for us, and Captain Allen Young had thoroughly carried out the kindly service volunteered by him.

With news but four months old on board, and only Melville Bay and the Atlantic between us and home, we felt that the Expedition was practically concluded. Melville Bay had been so rarely visited at this late season of the year that hardly anything was known about it. To our surprise we found it altogether free from pack-ice, a rolling sea of comparatively warm water, very green in colour, and swarming with microscopic animal life.

Our coal at last came to an end, and for fourteen days strong head-winds baffled us; day after day the two ships beat about in fog and storm, through fleets of icebergs that would have made us very uncomfortable if we had not learnt implicit confidence in our officers of the watches. Finally the weather moderated, and we reached Disco on 25th September. Every Eskimo that came on board looked like an old friend. We were most kindly received by all the inhabitants, from the Danish Inspector, who shared his small stock of coal with us, to the young urchins that kept us supplied with delicious fresh fish. Poor people! they were more in need of help from us than we were from them. The season had been a bad one, and scurvy was very prevalent both at Disco and Egedesminde. Even the little children looked miserably withered and weak, and we were glad to have some little remains of our mess stock to serve out amongst them.

At Disco we bade good-bye to our two trusty dog-drivers, Hans and Fred, and on 2nd October the Expedition set sail for England. The voyage home was one succession of gales; the Flying Dutchman himself could hardly have experienced worse weather. The ships soon lost sight of each other, and to complicate matters the "Alert's" rudder, which had never been strong since its last crush in the ice, gave way completely, and left her to make for the nearest port as best she could. On the 27th October she reached Valentia, and two days afterwards her consort, the "Discovery," anchored in Bantry Bay.

DEVICE ON DELF-WARE OF THE EXPEDITION